A Culinary History of
KENTUCKY

A Culinary History of

KENTUCKY

BURGOO, BEER CHEESE & GOETTA

· FIONA YOUNG-BROWN ·

AMERICAN PALATE

Published by American Palate
A Division of The History Press
Charleston, SC 29403
www.historypress.net

Cover image of Walter Kern pouring a Derby Pie® courtesy of Kern's Kitchen.

Images courtesy of the author unless otherwise noted.

First published 2014

Manufactured in the United States

ISBN 978.1.62619.263.8

Library of Congress CIP data applied for.

CONTENTS

Acknowledgements   7
Introduction   9

PART I: KENTUCKY BEGINNINGS   11
Settling Kentucky   11
The Kentucky Kitchen   18

PART II: FRUITS AND VEGETABLES   23
Corn   23
Beans   31
Messes of Greens   36
More than Just Greens   43
Apples: Custard, Crab and Cultivated   49

PART III: MEAT AND FISH   54
High on the Hog   54
Burgoo and Barbecue   60
Fried Chicken   67
Fish and Frogs   73

Contents

Part IV: Beverages   80

Bourbon and Moonshine   80
Sweet Tea and Sodey-Pop   88

Part V: Something Sweet   93
Sorghum: The Sweet Behind It All   93
Butter My Biscuits   97
Baked Goods   101
Desserts   109
Candies   115

Part VI: Kentucky Specialties   122

Part VII: The Future of Kentucky Food   132

Bibliography   135
Index   141
About the Author   143

ACKNOWLEDGEMENTS

As with any book project, there are many more people involved than I will probably remember to thank. However, I will do my best to express my gratitude to all those who have supported and helped me, both directly and indirectly.

First, I must thank my fellow Kentucky food bloggers, many of whom offered ideas, resources and suggestions. In particular, thanks to Maureen C. Berry for sharing her wonderful photographs, Rona Roberts for her knowledge of sorghum, Joyce Pinson for her knowledge of eastern Kentucky foodways and Michelle Turner for her sharing of custard recipes.

Thanks to those who helped me a few years back when I was researching a piece about the history of beer cheese for *Culture* magazine—Mark Sohn, Ronnie Lundy, John T. Edge and Sarah Fritschner. Little did I know at the time that it would feed my desire to learn more to the point that I would end up working on this book.

Many local restaurants and businesses helped by showing me their archives or facilities, sharing stories and more. The folks at Ale-8-One, Buffalo Trace, Old Hickory Bar-B-Q, Scott Hams, Smokey Pig, Kentucky State University and the Brown Hotel have all been very accommodating. Particular thanks go to Miss Dixie Huffman for her wonderful hospitality at Shaker Village in Pleasant Hill.

Several friends deserve special mention. Julie Quinn Blyth, Amanda Hervey and Neil Chethik—thank you all. Thanks to my husband Nic's family for sharing stories and recipes.

And lastly, thanks to Nic for offering advice and for putting up with me when I reach those last few weeks of pulling my hair out as I wonder if I will meet my deadline, as well as for being willing to try whatever dish I put in front of him.

INTRODUCTION

I experienced my first true taste of Kentucky in the summer of 1998 in the small town of Barbourville, where I was meeting my future in-laws. Mashed potatoes and gravy, ham, fried chicken, corn, deviled eggs, corn bread and freshly baked rolls were piled high on plates, accompanied by the green beans that had been furiously hissing in the pressure cooker. As my plate emptied, I was urged to help myself to more, but I dared not, having already spied the several types of pie that would serve as a more than ample dessert.

In the years since then, I have eaten many similar meals, and my appreciation for what appeared at first to be a very simple meal has grown immensely. The vegetables were all grown and harvested on the family farm, with the remainder baked in the ever-busy kitchen, using recipes that have been passed down through the generations. Much of the preparation has changed little since Rebecca Boone and the early pioneers learned to live on what the land provided. And provide it did. From the forests and mountains of Appalachia in the east to the rivers and pastures of the west, Kentucky is a natural cornucopia of deliciousness, offering fruits, vegetables, fish and fowl.

But it took me time to appreciate its rich abundance and simplicity. During my first weeks in the state, I happened to tune in to a radio interview with a few local farmers. They were discussing the harvest of peppers and zucchini blossoms. What should one do with these gems, asked the interviewer? Batter and fry them of course, came the reply. My heart sank, as it seemed that once again, the stereotype of Kentucky—and perhaps most southern—food as anything that can be battered and fried had reared its ugly head. Mention the word "Kentucky," and no matter where you are in the world, people think of fried chicken. Greasy, fast-food chicken. In truth, Kentucky food is much more than that, and the fried chicken—*proper* fried chicken—is moist and flavorful, prepared with a skill that no fast-food restaurant can replicate.

My husband likes to tell me that food is how Kentuckians show their love. He may well be right, for there is an undeniable social value in the sharing of a meal here in the commonwealth. I defy you to visit any part of the state and not be offered, at the very least, a glass of tea, some fresh biscuits or a piece of chess pie. Holidays and reunions are centered on the intersection of food and family, and even in this age of convenience foods and TV dinners, mealtimes in much of Kentucky are still a vital time of coming together. As noted historian Thomas D. Clark wrote, "Eating dinner in Kentucky is more than a physiological refueling of the human body; it is a joyous social ritual."

So what is Kentucky food? ("Cuisine" seems far too pretentious a term for something so richly based in the region's fertile ground.) To quote Marion Flexner, "Kentucky cooking is a unique blend of many old-world cultures seasoned with native ingenuity, a cross section of American cookery at its best." Kentucky cooking is a collective memory of every pioneer who ever crossed the Cumberland Gap, every immigrant who settled here and every native who lived here before that. It is simple yet complex in its origins. It is more than a meal on a plate. It is community. It is hospitality. It is history.

Note: It will be somewhat inevitable that some readers will not find a particular Kentucky favorite mentioned within these pages. While I have attempted to paint a broad picture of Kentucky foodways, this book is not intended to be a complete survey of the state's eating habits and recipes. Rather, it is a collection of historical tales and trivia about where some of our dishes come from. In looking at the influences behind our food, I hope to also show how the generations of settlers and immigrants from various cultures have taken those dishes and adapted them to become something that is uniquely Kentucky.

PART I
KENTUCKY BEGINNINGS

SETTLING KENTUCKY

In 1750, Dr. Thomas Walker "discovered" the Cumberland Gap, a passage through the Appalachian Mountains from Virginia. A replica of the cabin he constructed can be seen at the Dr. Thomas Walker State Historic Site in Barbourville. A small fort, built in 1769, was soon abandoned, but six years later, Daniel Boone led a group of thirty loggers along the trail, often termed the Wilderness Road. Hired by the Transylvania Company, he and his companions would widen the path for the thousands of men, women and wagons that would eventually cross; some estimates claim that as many as 300,000 had crossed the Cumberland Gap by 1810. Unlike the first settlers in Jamestown and New England, who were not skilled as huntsmen and fishermen and therefore frequently starved despite the plethora of food sources, these pioneers were of much more rugged and hardy stock. Some would continue farther west, beyond the Mississippi, but most would settle and tame the wild frontier that was to become Kentucky. It would be all too easy to talk about Kentucky food as something that developed from that point on. To do so, however, would be to ignore one of the main—or indeed *the* main—influences on the region's eating habits.

Few visible geographic markers remain to indicate Kentucky's Indian heritage, but our dining tables are constant reminders of the edible bounty that existed here long before the pioneers arrived, a bounty that fed the Cherokees and Shawnees, who, while not permanent inhabitants of the area, sent hunting parties regularly. Why send hunting parties if there wasn't some good food to be found? Kentucky was a virtual supermarket of abundance. The Chickasaws and Creeks, as well as those already mentioned, knew that Kentucky was a rich source of food, and many of those foods have since made their way into our diet. Although long since gone, the flats of central and western Kentucky were once roaming grounds for buffalo. It is no coincidence that Buffalo Trace is so named; the distillery is located at one of the spots carved out by generations of buffalo migration before the animals were eventually driven farther west by encroaching settlers. Other sources of readily available meat included deer, turkey, squirrel and opossum. Then there were the nuts, squash, wild greens, beans and corn that all thrived in the local climate. It is no surprise that so many Kentucky dishes are rooted in the traditions of the Native American peoples who once passed through these lands. The earliest forms of corn bread, hoecakes and poke sallet—some even claim perhaps burgoo—were all produced with what was readily available and a fire.

The Scotch-Irish were highly influential in both the settlement of Kentucky and the development of Kentucky cooking. According to the Merriam-Webster dictionary, the first known use of the name "Scotch-Irish" was in 1744, and the phrase is of American origin. However, it is known to have been used before that; Elizabeth I of England used it in a letter written in 1573. The term was also none too complimentary. In the seventeenth century, the British began to colonize Northern Ireland through the Plantation of Ulster. King James I decided that the plantation would bring a civilizing (i.e. Protestant) influence to the largely Catholic, Gaelic-speaking land. Wealthy Scottish Presbyterians and members of the Church of England were offered land that had been confiscated from Irish chieftains. Having been banned from employing Irish workers or tenants, they then were required to bring more Scots and English across the sea. Although one requirement was that the settlers spoke English, it is now believed that a large number of those from Scotland spoke Gaelic also. As it happened, given the proximity of Ireland and Scotland, there was already a sizeable Scottish population in Ulster. Following the plantation, however, they arrived in larger numbers.

Harvesting potatoes in rural Jefferson County. *Library of Congress.*

One failing of the scheme was that the planned colonization coincided with the settlement of Jamestown and subsequent migration to the New World. This saw a good number of English crossing the Atlantic rather than settling in Ulster.

But what of the Scotch-Irish? Those who arrived in the first American colonies from Ulster referred to themselves as Irish. It was these people who settled much of Appalachia; those who fought against the British in the Revolution were paid for their military service with tracts of land in the as-yet-undeveloped region. Only later, when the floods of Irish immigrants fled the potato famine and came to American shores, did those already settled here for generations adopt the name Scotch-Irish as a means of distinguishing themselves from the new arrivals. Describing oneself or one's ancestors as Scotch-Irish is very much an Americanism. Natives of Scotland refer to themselves as Scottish or Scots, never Scotch. Both the Scottish and Irish sometimes find the term offensive, denoting something that does not exist. Nevertheless, in the United States, Scotch-Irish is a name that has endured for several centuries. Whether those first Scotch-Irish settlers in Appalachia were of Scottish descent, having lived in Ulster for only a few decades before migrating, or were of true Irish descent, we may never know.

Fortunately for us, their influence on Kentucky's food heritage is much easier to pinpoint. In addition to potatoes, they brought a number of key foodstuffs

Example of a pioneer kitchen at Old Fort Harrod. *Louis Edward Nollau Nitrate Photographic Print Collection, University of Kentucky.*

with them—or at least adaptations thereof. Whereas oats were a staple in Scotland, in the New World, corn took their place. Jay Anderson, a professor emeritus of history at Utah State University who specializes in foodways, noted that "[t]he Scots' mastery of corn was total." Oatmeal porridge was replaced by cornmush or grits, bread recipes used the new grain and other recipes changed in a similar fashion. Steamed puddings and thick, hearty stews were from the Scottish peasant tradition, as was the skill at foraging for wild greens. The Scots and Irish also had a love of dairy products, and butter and buttermilk made regular appearances at the table. And let's not forget the continuation of the distilling tradition with bourbon whiskey.

Despite what sometimes seems to be an unwavering determination by every Kentuckian to declare Scotch-Irish and Cherokee heritage, the English contributions to the state's food habits should not be ignored. Their influence is equally strong, and indeed, since relocating here, I am frequently surprised by the number of "traditional Appalachian" foods or phrases that I grew up with in the south of England. The saying may claim to be "as American as apple pie," but the recipe is all English. Many English immigrated from East Anglia and the Midlands, settling first in Virginia, the Carolinas and

Pennsylvania before making their way across the Cumberland Gap. With them they brought their knowledge and skill in food preservation. Country hams, cured meats, pickles and butters all have their roots in the British Isles, as do a number of cakes, puddings and pastries, not to mention a love of roast meats and fried fish. The Romans introduced pigs to the British centuries earlier, and while many Scots refused to eat pork, hogs were a staple farther south. Combined with Indian corn, pork would become a staple in the American South too. While on the subject of staples, the Scots may have made bourbon their lasting legacy to the state, but where would we be without moonshine or the mint julep (both of English origin)?

Whereas the rugged terrain of eastern Kentucky matched that of the Scottish Highlands, the central and western parts of the state were more reminiscent of England and thus were well suited to English-style farming, with fruit orchards and grazing lands.

Other influences are also apparent, some in Southern cooking as a whole, some strictly in Kentucky cooking and some in hyperlocalized dishes. African slaves, Germans, Dutch, French and, in more recent times, Latino immigrants have all made their mark.

The Shakers

Kentucky not only provided a new home for various ethnic groups but also offered land and a new start for some religious groups. One of these groups kept detailed records of its purchases, farming and community life—enough that we can see how people lived on a daily basis.

This particular group has its roots in Manchester, England, the birthplace of Ann Lees, who would later become more widely known as Mother Ann Lee. Although raised a Quaker, at the age of twenty-two she joined a breakaway group that, inspired by a small sect of French Calvinists, would enter trances as a means of worship. Often these trances would cause them to shake in a seemingly uncontrollable manner. They became known as the Shaking Quakers, or Shakers. Following the deaths of all four of her children, Ann became convinced that cohabitation was a cardinal sin and that celibacy was the only way to live. She was imprisoned for a while before sailing to the New World with a small group of followers. Eventually, a number of Shaker communities formed throughout New England, all modeled around a working, celibate community that relied on adoption of orphans and recruitment of new members to keep numbers strong.

Shaker Village at Pleasant Hill continues to attract visitors with its fine food. *Postcard Collection at the University of Kentucky.*

In 1805, three Shaker missionaries entered Kentucky with the intention of seeking new converts and building a new community. The following year, land covenants were signed, and Pleasant Hill was created (the community bound itself in a formal covenant in 1814). Over time, more lands were added, and soon the Shaker community at Pleasant Hill occupied more than four thousand acres. A second community that eventually covered more than six thousand acres was formed in 1807 in South Union. The South Union community remained active until 1922, Pleasant Hill until 1910.

Members of both Shaker communities raised their own food and ate what they produced: fruit, vegetables, dairy produce, cattle, hogs and more. Sheep were raised for wool and for mutton. Fish could be caught within the community grounds. The variety of potential foodstuffs was much more extensive than we tend to imagine today. The Shaker diet did not differ greatly from their non-Shaker neighbors, but their meticulous recordkeeping makes it easy to develop a strong picture of the typical daily diet of the nineteenth-century Kentuckian: locally grown and raised food. Interestingly, they did make occasional alterations to their diet for health reasons. In the mid-1850s, pork was banned for a ten-year period, as it was considered unhealthy. Fortunately, they soon saw the folly in their avoidance of bacon and reintroduced one of Kentucky's staples to their plates. They also briefly banned tea and coffee, but one suspects the caffeine withdrawal proved unbearable.

Preserving for winter was a vital part of food preparation, and so canning, drying, salting and pickling were skills possessed by the average woman, Shaker or not. Some jams and sweetmeats were preserved for use within the community (and therefore were kept in pottery jars). Others were preserved in glass jars for sale to outsiders. Every fall, once the flurry of activity to preserve the harvest was complete, some of the Shaker men would travel south to buy sugar and lemons (attempts to grow their own Chinese sorghum had failed, so sugar was an important purchase). No doubt they would take some of their preserves to trade. Both sugar and lemons would be used to make a dessert that remains popular to this day among visitors to Shaker Village at Pleasant Hill.

Shaker Lemon Pie
(as Shared in Caroline B. Piercy's The Shaker Cook Book)

When thinking of lemon pie, we tend to envisage a lemon meringue. The Shaker version of lemon pie is quite different, making use of the entire lemon, peel and all. Careful preparation of the lemons and judicious use of sugar results in a deliciously tart yet sweet dessert.

2 large lemons
2 cups sugar
4 eggs, beaten
2 pie crusts

Slice the lemons as thinly as possible, complete with the rinds. A mandoline is perhaps the best tool to ensure very thin slices. Cover the lemon slices with the sugar and mix, taking care not to crush the fruit. Leave to stand overnight. Add the beaten eggs and stir. Use one pie crust to line a 9-inch pie plate. Arrange the lemon slice mixture in the pie base and cover with the second pastry crust. Make a few slits in the pie crust for any air to escape. Bake at 450° F for 15 minutes. Then, reduce the heat to 375° F and continue to cook for a further 20 minutes.

THE KENTUCKY KITCHEN

The Kentucky cook was skillful. She, for it was usually a woman, might be responsible for harvesting vegetables, skinning animals, fetching water, doing laundry, making soap, chopping wood and building fires even before she got around to the actual cooking of the dinner. Furthermore, she relied on just a few basic utensils that were capable of meeting everyday cooking needs. The tools of the pioneer kitchen were a far cry from today's technological timesaving wonders.

In the earliest (and later, the poorest) cabins, one room would serve as kitchen, dining room and sleeping quarters. The fireplace provided both cooking space and warmth. Only in larger plantations could one expect to find a series of exterior buildings quite separate from the main living space. These might include a smokehouse and a bake house so that the smells of food preparation and preservation would not impose on the sensibilities of the plantation mistress.

Dr. Daniel Drake, who would later teach medicine at both Transylvania University and the Louisville Medical College, grew up in a poor frontier family who moved to Kentucky when he was just three years old. His later recollections in *Pioneer Life in Kentucky* paint a picture of a typical Kentucky kitchen:

> *I know of no scene in civilized life more primitive than such a cabin hearth as that of my mother. In the morning, a buckeye backlog and hickory forestick resting on stone andirons, with a Jonny cake on a clean ash board, set before it to bake, a frying pan with its long handle resting on a split bottomed turner's chair…and the tea kettle swung from a wooden "lug pole" with myself setting the table, or turning the meat or watching the Jonny cake, while she sat nursing the baby.*

Early fireplaces relied on a simple pole—known as a lug pole—positioned above the fire, from which cooking pots could hang. They were originally made of fresh-cut wood, which over time would dry and char, often breaking and sending the cooking pot splashing into the fire. Burns and scaldings were all too common. Thus, wooden poles, which clearly were not the safest idea above an open flame, eventually gave way to iron. Later, various hinges, cranes and pulley systems replaced the basic pole. These allowed the cook to handle pots without having to lean over the flames. Temperature control

Churning butter was just one of the many duties of a Kentucky wife. *Marion Post Wolcott, Library of Congress.*

A typical farming family from Rockcastle County in 1916. *Lewis Wickes Hine, Library of Congress.*

relied on different-sized hooks to raise the pots closer to or farther away from the fire, as well as the experience of the cook.

Ovens were a different matter altogether. In the pioneer kitchen, the fireplace was the only cook-space. This also helps to explain why corn bread was made in a skillet over the fire and why, in some rural areas, biscuits and other baked goods did not become popular until well into the twentieth century. Larger houses might also have a brick oven built into a wall. These would later become commonly known as beehive ovens. However, the use of the beehive oven required a lot of time, skill and preparation, and they were used only for breads and pastries. Meat would be cooked over the fire. The cook needed to keep a watchful eye on her baking, moving items based on what seemed to be the hottest spots. The fire had to be started early in the morning, and by the time the oven was suitably hot—the breads were baked then—it was usually nightfall. And the oven still had to be swept clean. Thus, baking was often restricted to one day per week. In some of the poorest parts of eastern Kentucky, people remained reliant on cooking over an open fire several decades into the twentieth century, well after their richer neighbors had bought stoves and ovens.

Cooking utensils would have been made of wood (basic spoons and trenchers), iron (pots and skillets) and tin (plates and mugs). Long-handed wooden peels would be used to place breads in the oven and to remove them when done. Cast-iron cookware remains a key feature even in today's modern kitchens, with many cooks continuing to use the skillets or Dutch ovens passed down from their grandmothers. Their appeal goes beyond their durability and versatility. A cast-iron skillet that has served several generations is a very personal link to the past, and to use someone else's cast iron seems almost like invading another's private history. Andrea King Collier's grandmother saw her cookware as other members of the family, even with their own names. Their cast-iron nature made them survivors, a reminder of the strong women in the author's past, her legacy. Many cooks also insist that each piece of cast iron takes on its own flavor over time, a personal seasoning.

Lastly, there was the issue of storing food so that it did not spoil—milk and eggs, for instance. First, we must remember that the average pioneer family, even if they had access to a cow for milk, would not have had a large supply. It would usually be consumed before it had time to spoil. If it needed to be kept until supper time, many would use a method still in use in the 1930s: keeping it in the coolest place possible, usually a well. It could be placed there in a bucket in the morning after milking and stay until it was used later in the day. The pioneer housewife was also expected to know all about preserving, pickling, curing, drying and salting, and a root cellar of some sort usually existed, often dug into the ground beside the house.

Martha McCulloch-Williams recommended the use of rainwater when making a brine for pickling. Among items she suggested for pickling in brine were watermelon rinds, beans, squash, peppers and cucumbers.

Mary Harris Frazer's Tomato Pickles

One peck of green tomatoes, 6 green peppers, remove seed, 6 large white onions. Chop these ingredients and sprinkle over it 1 cup of salt, let remain one night. In morning drain well, add 2 cups of sugar, spices of all kind (put in a bag), and vinegar to cover it well and ¼ pound white mustard seed, boil tomatoes until quite soft, put in jar, tie up securely.

Even in the first half of the twentieth century, rural women often held responsibilities both inside and outside the home. We tend to think of women working outside the home as a relatively recent development, since 1950 or so, but doing so discounts the immense amount of labor put in by women on family farms. Meals and cooking had to be based around the times when the women of the household would be gone into the fields to work on the planting and harvesting. Once the household labors were done, out to the garden or fields they went. In *Food and Everyday Life on Kentucky Family Farms, 1920–1950*, John and Anne van Willigen gave a detailed look at the lives of typical farm families in Kentucky during the pre–World War II years. Breakfast was a large meal, providing energy for the working day. It often consisted of eggs, biscuits, gravy, tomatoes and some sort of meat, perhaps ham, bacon or even chicken fried steak if a big day of work lay ahead—a far cry from today's hurried slice of toast or bowl of cereal.

The midday meal was usually the largest meal of the day for several reasons. It provided further energy for the afternoon's labors, the fires from the stove would keep the house nicely heated for evening but not overly heated through the night (particularly in summer) and, lastly, the lack of refrigerated storage allowed for the leftovers to be eaten as supper, thereby leaving little waste. As a result of these demands, women—be they the earliest pioneers or twentieth-century farm wives—would cook meals that could be left to cook slowly while they were engaged elsewhere. There was too much to be done to spend hours in the kitchen preparing something fancy by modern standards. A large kettle of soup beans, green beans with ham or stew could be left to cook all morning. By midday, it would be ready to accompany the rest of the dinner, which often included potatoes, corn, corn bread and meat, usually pork or chicken. Any leftovers would be enjoyed for supper.

PART II
FRUITS AND VEGETABLES

CORN

Corn may be the lifeblood of the Midwest's agrarian economy, but in the South it is religion.

—Ronni Lundy, Butter Beans to Blackberries

If there is one food that truly stands out as an example of Old World ingenuity adapting New World ingredients, it has to be that staple of pioneer food: corn. It is, without a doubt, the most important foodstuff in the history of America, from the Pilgrims on the New England coast to the vast expanses of Kansas and Nebraska. Lyn Kellner likened its importance to that of rice in China.

For generations, long before the arrival of white settlers, Native Americans knew of the potential within corn (also known as maize). In fact, archaeologists have found evidence that Central American natives used special techniques to cultivate and develop the indigenous plant into what we would recognize today. The ears of corn on the earliest plants (known as *teosinte*) were quite small, just a few inches in length and containing only a few kernels. Understanding the nutritional and culinary possibilities, early farmers cultivated the plants in such a way that over the next few thousand years, the ears (and thus the yield) grew in size. As the crop grew, so did its usefulness as a dietary staple. At the same time, the cultivation of corn spread among other tribes, eventually finding its way as far north as New England, which is where the Pilgrims first encountered it. By the time the Europeans arrived, the local tribes had found multiple uses for corn: hominy, succotash and cornmeal mush were all regular eats, while the husks were woven into mats or used to make dolls or even footwear. The leftover cobs were used to fashion pipes.

When white settlers first arrived, they were determined to grow crops similar to those they had cultivated in the Old World. However, they soon found that oats and wheat were not easily grown in the land now available to them. Corn, on the other hand, could be grown on even the smallest patch of land, and it could be used in a multiplicity of ways. Immigrants soon learned how to cultivate it and use it in their kitchens. Indeed, historians have often speculated that, had they not learned to do so, they may never have colonized the continent. Corn also provided food for the hogs (thus extending its use as a food source), and let us not forget its later contributions to distillation.

Among the main types of corn, we have sweet corn (probably the best known), hominy corn (with its large kernels), flint corn, flour corn and dent corn. The last is also referred to as field corn or feed corn and can be found in southern kitchens as hominy, grits and cornmeal. Sweet corn is most commonly used as a vegetable, although Rick McDaniel noted that this usage did not come about until the early twentieth century. Long before its place among the vegetable dishes, corn was first and foremost a grain.

The earliest form of corn bread was known as cornpone or apon, and it was taught to early settlers by the local Native Americans. It was made by simply mixing cornmeal and water and then frying in fat. Cornmeal mush used the same two ingredients, but instead of frying, the mix was cooked in a way similar to porridge or oatmeal and could be sweetened with honey or molasses. Later, European ingredients were added—eggs, milk, butter and salt. Corn bread was a fixture at every meal, no matter how rich or poor you might be. But even corn bread can count a variety of culinary kin: cornpone, johnnycakes, hush puppies, corn muffins and spoonbread, to name just a few.

In the *Rebecca Boone Cook Book*, Clark County native Bertha Barnes shared an assortment of recipes handed down by the descendants of the first settlers at Fort Boonesborough. She speculated that many of these recipes may be those used by Daniel Boone's wife and other early pioneers. In this brief pamphlet alone, one can find instructions on making cornpone, corn sticks and multiple versions of corn bread. Corn was most likely on the menu at least twice a day, and if you had nothing else in the way of food, you could always scrape together some corn mush. Otis Rice noted that "any housewife who could not prepare a variety of tasty corn dishes could hardly qualify as a cook."

When settlers moved into what is now Kentucky (then part of Virginia), the Virginia State Assembly passed a 1776 land law governing who should be allowed to claim land: "[N]o family shall be entitled to the allowance granted to settlers…unless they have made a crop of corn in that country, or resided there at least one year." In 1779, for a price of ten dollars, the assembly offered four hundred acres of Kentucky land to any person who would settle the land, build a residence and plant a corn crop on the land within a year. Such laws indicate the importance of corn, not just as daily sustenance but also as a means of expanding territory and the economy. Revered Kentucky historian Thomas D. Clark wrote, "Kentucky River people have eaten corn bread since the first day a white man kindled his campfire in the valley. Corn bread is as necessary a part of their diet as is salt." He recognized that corn has forever been a symbol of food for the people of the commonwealth, and even the simplest version of corn bread—just meal, water and salt—could be "a glorious asset to a good vegetable dinner."

Mrs. Fisher's Plantation Corn Bread or Hoe Cake

Half tablespoonful of lard to a pint of meal, one teacup of boiling water; stir well and bake on a hot griddle. Sift in meal one teaspoonful of soda.

When it comes to corn bread, most southern cooks stand united: it should never contain sugar. Indeed, to once more quote Ronni Lundy, self-proclaimed corn bread fundamentalist: "If God had meant for cornbread to have sugar in it, he'd have called it cake." Traditional corn bread, like most Kentucky home cooking, requires only the most simple of ingredients and tools, but to substitute just one of them throws the entire dish off balance. The tools required are a cast-iron skillet, bacon grease and a hot oven; the ingredients are offered below. (As an aside, no self-respecting Kentucky cook is without a jar of bacon grease in her kitchen that is constantly being used and refilled.)

The Canary Cottage restaurant chain was based in Lexington. A 1938 menu special included southern corn fritters with maple syrup, bacon and coffee for thirty-five cents. *Postcard Collection at the University of Kentucky.*

Basic Corn Bread

¼ cup bacon grease
1 cup cornmeal
1 tablespoon baking powder
1 teaspoon baking soda
1 teaspoon salt
1 egg
1 cup flour
1⅓ cups buttermilk

Preheat the oven to 450° F. Place the bacon grease in an iron skillet and melt in the hot oven.

Mix together the remaining ingredients. Once the grease is melted and the oven is at the right temperature, pour the bacon grease into the corn bread mix. Stir and pour back into the skillet. Bake for 25 minutes until crisp and golden.

Flourless Corn Bread

This recipe is similar to the one aforementioned but does not use any flour. As such, it is probably much closer to what the earliest settlers at Boonesboro would have made (albeit on a fire instead of in an oven).

bacon grease or lard
1 cup cornmeal
1 egg
1 cup buttermilk
pinch of salt

Preheat oven to 500° F. Melt enough bacon grease in a skillet to have a depth of about half an inch. Mix the cornmeal, egg, buttermilk and salt. Pour the melted grease into the mixing bowl. Stir with the cornmeal and return the mix to the hot skillet. Bake for 10 to 15 minutes.

Of course, how you choose to eat your corn bread once it's cooked is a matter of personal preference, but as you will often find in Kentucky and indeed southern cooking, that preference may just be the source of many a harsh debate. Some people like theirs with a spread of butter and nothing more. Others enjoy it with soup beans or pot likker/liquor—the broth left from cooking greens—but whether to crumble into the bowl, dip carefully or place in the bottom of the bowl and pour the likker on top is a matter known to bring men to blows.

Reputedly, Huey Long, the fiery Louisiana governor and inspiration for Kentuckian Robert Penn Warren's *All the King's Men*, was an outspoken proponent of dunking his corn bread into his pot likker as opposed to crumbling, an act he considered most ill-mannered. This seems a reasonable enough statement of a personal preference, but in 1930, this was enough to cause quite the journalistic uproar. The editor of the *Atlanta Constitution* wrote an editorial claiming that anyone would know that crumbling is the only way to eat corn bread and likker. In a move that perhaps only those acquainted with the importance of honor to the southern gentleman can truly appreciate, the editor also wrote of his belief that Long must crumble in private. The governor responded that such an accusation was the worst form of journalism. Whether the exchange was truly antagonistic or merely mild-humored, it serves to illustrate the almost religious devotion to corn bread and eating habits.

Corn bread and a bowl of soup beans remains a hearty favorite among many eastern Kentuckians, a simple, warming and nutritious dish that is suitable for any day of the week. My husband tells of his grandmother's nightly ritual of making a skillet of corn bread to enjoy with a glass of buttermilk as she watched television. There was no finer meal to finish the day, and one suspects that this same ritual meal had been enjoyed many decades earlier during her childhood in Clay County.

Yet even corn bread can be elevated to high cuisine. Raymond Sokolov referred to spoonbread as "the highest form of corn bread…a cryptosoufflé." Rick McDaniel described it as a "fusion of three cultures"—Native American corn meets a French soufflé at the hand of an African American cook. The dish is thought by some to have originated in Virginia in the 1820s, while others argue that it was created during the Civil War era. Regardless of its origin, the name "spoonbread" did not appear in print until the dawn of the twentieth century; Martha McCulloch-Williams included a recipe for "Mush Bread," noting that some call it "Spoon bread." Today, Berea's Boone Tavern Hotel is considered *the* place to go for spoonbread. The town even hosts an annual festival dedicated to it. Spoonbread, as the name suggests, cannot be eaten by hand. It is a light, fluffy dish, often served instead of potatoes or as an additional side.

Spoonbread

4 tablespoons butter
3 cups milk
1¼ cups ground cornmeal
1 teaspoon baking powder
1 teaspoon salt
2 eggs, beaten

Use 1 tablespoon of the butter to grease either a cake pan or a cast-iron skillet.

Bring the milk to a boil over a high heat. Add the cornmeal to the boiling milk, stirring all the while to blend the two ingredients. Remove from the heat and cool to room temperature. Once the mixture has cooled, add the remaining 3 tablespoons of butter (melted), the baking powder, the salt and the beaten eggs. Using either a mixer or by hand, whisk vigorously for about 15 minutes.

Pour the batter into the pan and bake in a preheated oven (350° F) for about 1 hour and 20 minutes. When cooked, the spoonbread should be golden and fluffy. As with any soufflé, spoonbread should be served immediately.

Midway's Weisenberger Mill has been grinding corn, grits and flour since 1865. *Weisenberger Mill.*

Despite its regional popularity, spoonbread has never surpassed corn bread, indicating that when it comes to Kentucky food, simple is best.

Grits never seem to have caught on in Kentucky with the same voracity as farther south. To be true, there are Kentuckians who relish eating them every day, be it with butter for breakfast or with cheese as an accompaniment to dinner. But compared to elsewhere, places where grits are a standard on every menu, they just don't compare to corn bread or biscuits for many folks in the Bluegrass. Weisenberger Mills, in Scott County, has produced old-fashioned stone-ground grits, along with wheat flour and cornmeal, since the nineteenth century. The mill, situated on the South Elkhorn Creek, has been operated by six generations of the Weisenberger family, descended from August, who arrived from Germany in 1862 and purchased the mill just a few years later. Their grits remain the best known in Kentucky.

Grits

4 cups water
1 cup stone ground grits

Bring the water to a boil. Add the grits and reduce the heat. Cover and allow to cook for about 25 minutes, stirring as needed. The cooked grits may be eaten as is, with just a touch of salt, or they may be mixed with cheese. Food writer John Egerton suggests shaping any leftover cold grits into patties and frying them in pork drippings.

Fresh sweet corn is a joy to eat, and at harvest time in Kentucky, there is no need to visit the grocery store when farmers' market stalls and roadside stands are piled high with corn picked so recently that all it needs for perfect enjoyment is the briefest time in boiling water. It is still referred to by many as "rosineers" (roasting ears) since it can be cooked on the fire or grill as easily as it can be boiled. For those wishing an alternative to straight from the cob, or for those times of the year when freshly picked corn is not available and one has to rely on frozen, creamed corn is a favorite option.

Creamed Corn

The sugar in this recipe is optional. In fresh corn, the natural sugars will be enough to sweeten the dish; however, for frozen corn, a little additional sweetness may be necessary.

6 to 8 ears of corn (or the frozen equivalent)
2 tablespoons butter or bacon grease
1 tablespoon flour
½ teaspoon salt
½ teaspoon pepper
1 cup cream (milk may be used but skim milk will not produced a
    good level of creaminess)
¼ cup water
1 tablespoon sugar (optional)

Carefully cut the kernels of corn from the cobs and scrape the cobs to remove any extra "milk." In an iron skillet, melt the grease or butter over a medium heat. Add the corn and corn milk. Stir in the flour, salt, pepper, cream and water (and sugar, if used). Simmer for 20 to 30 minutes, until it reaches the preferred thickness. Add extra salt and pepper to taste.

BEANS

In the 1949 chart-topping song by Louis Jordan and the Tympany Five, that beloved food twosome beans and corn bread get into a fight. After going a few rounds of knock-down brawling, the two realize that they belong together like, well, beans and corn bread.

A bowl of soup beans mopped up with freshly baked corn bread is still a popular and warming supper in much of eastern Kentucky. Truth be told, Kentuckians have raised beans beyond a mere vegetable or legume to a culinary art form. Entire books have been written on the bean varieties to be found in Kentucky.

Beans are by no means a New World discovery. Beans and pulses were an important part of potage, the daily stew eaten by many medieval peasants throughout Europe. The beans they would have enjoyed were a variety of broad bean (what Americans know as a fava bean). Since they grew wild (having been introduced from North Africa), the beans could be gathered along with wild greens and left to stew for supper. A fourteenth-century recipe for "Drawen Benes" is similar to a basic bean soup that one might eat today, the only noticeable differences being the use of saffron and the lack of ham.

Drawen Benes

2 cups broth
16 ounces fava beans, cooked and lightly mashed
1 large onion, roughly chopped
1 pinch saffron
salt

Bring the broth to a boil. Add the beans, onion and saffron. Cook until the onions are soft and translucent. Add salt to taste.

Kentucky Soup Beans

1 pound pinto beans (any other dried bean can also be used)
12 cups water
ham hock
1 onion, peeled
1 clove garlic, peeled
½ teaspoon salt
1 teaspoon pepper

Put all of the ingredients in a large Dutch oven and bring to a boil. Lower the heat and simmer for 1½ to 2 hours, adding more water if necessary. Remove from the heat and discard the onion and garlic. Remove 2 cups of the beans; place them in a bowl and mash lightly. Return them to the pot and serve the soup beans with corn bread.

The early European immigrants found an array of American bean species when they landed in North America. Much as African species had made their way into Europe, so had South American species made their way farther north. Native Americans had long since learned that beans and corn paired well; they planted them together, allowing the beans to provide nitrogen to the corn while the corn offered a climbing frame for the beans. The two shared a symbiotic growing relationship. The similarities between European and American beans made the local varieties instantly recognizable among immigrants. They also brought varieties with them from Europe to plant, with varying degrees of success.

Modern beans fall into several categories: bush, pole, half runners and dried beans. To Kentuckians, particularly those in the Eastern part of the state, the latter are better known as shucky beans or leatherbritches. To the outsider, they appear to be little more than overdried, leathery-looking pieces of who-knows-what, way beyond the realms of something you might find on your dinner plate. To the trained eye, however, a jar of shucky beans is a feast in the making.

The term "leatherbritches" is possibly derived from the German *getrocken bohne* (a name given to dried string beans). In parts of Germany, it has been a practice since at least the fourteenth century to preserve beans for later use by drying them. When needed, they would be cooked for several hours in broth with a little meat for a healthful peasant dish. As with hog killing, canning and other aspects of harvest, the preparation of leatherbritches was

Eating has always been a social activity in Kentucky. These women share lunch during a break from their canning class. *Library of Congress.*

an important household ritual, key to ensuring that there would be a decent supply of food for the coming winter months.

Many Kentucky writers have recalled the work involved in threading the beans and leaving long strings of them to dry, often hanging from the edge of the porch. Half-runner beans of the white and mountain varieties were preferred by many for drying. Knowing when the beans were ready was half the battle—the pods should contain nicely sized, plump beans but should not be so old that they had grown tough. The ends of the pods should be snapped and the strings pulled off. Using a needle, the pods were then threaded onto a long length of twine, with care being taken to thread only through the pod and not through any of the beans themselves. Some people soaked the long rows of beans in a brine to help keep bugs away. They were then hung to dry. Folks often disagreed as to whether they should be hung in the sunlight or a more shady spot, but the most important part seems to have been that they were not subject to humidity, which would cause the beans to rot rather than dry. Once dried, the pods were removed from the threads and stored in jars or cans.

Billy Clark praised the versatility of the string bean (and its ability to be dried and stored) and noted that "stringless green beans were not considered worth planting in the hill country and were never tolerated. Not then, not now, by true country hill people." Such words speak of the continuing importance of beans in the Appalachian part of Kentucky.

So integral a part of Kentucky foodways are beans that they are eaten on New Year's Day to bring good luck. Many Kentuckians still enjoy the traditional January 1 meal of hog jowls, black-eyed peas and cabbage (or some other green), along with thousands throughout the South.

There are several explanations as to how this meal came about and why these specific ingredients are included. Some claim that black-eyed peas were once considered animal feed. During the Civil War, General William T. Sherman marched his Union troops through the South, raiding any food supplies they came across. All they supposedly left behind were the beans that were fit only for animals and the salted pork. Left with only these few rations to last the winter, they supposedly became symbols of good luck. Although this is certainly possible, I'm not entirely sure how this would have come to be the case in Kentucky, particularly since living on pork would hardly have been considered a hardship.

Another explanation is that black-eyed peas were a slave dish and that as the Emancipation Proclamation went into effect on January 1, 1863, slaves ate them in celebration. From that point on, they came to represent good luck. Again a plausible story, but that does not explain the dish's popularity among whites. A more basic reasoning is that the beans fared well against harsh winter weather and therefore were readily available.

Beans have been a symbol of good luck around the world for centuries. In Japan, the Setsubun Festival marks the arrival of spring and the ending of an old year with the eating of beans—one to represent each year of your life so far and another to bring luck in the coming year. Beans are also thrown out the door to keep bad luck or demons at bay. The fava bean is often carried as a good luck charm in Italy, and it is a traditional decoration for St. Joseph's Day celebrations. But the role of beans as a good luck symbol dates back even farther—to the Aztecs and the ancient Egyptians. In Egypt, they represented life, while in ancient Rome, the names of the key families could be linked to varieties of bean. Some records indicate that the Jews have eaten black-eyed peas at Rosh Hashana (Jewish New Year) for several millennia; in fact, some have suggested that the practice

The Jefferson County Community Cannery taught lessons in preserving vegetables for winter. This woman loads her car with freshly canned beans. *Library of Congress.*

of eating them at New Year in the South was influenced by Southern Jewish populations during the Civil War.

Whatever legend you choose to believe, black-eyed peas are likely to be forever a part of the Kentucky tradition for New Year. You may choose to eat 365 beans (for each day of the coming year), but if that seems excessive, some people simply eat the beans given to them, regardless of number. For some, the beans alone are enough, but in many households, they must have the traditional accompaniments to truly bring good fortune, and that includes hog jowls and greens. In our family, it is cabbage; in others, it is collard or turnip greens. It is said that the leaves of the greens are to represent money (and indeed some superstitions liken the beans to coins).

The fat of the pork represents prosperity, and like the bean, the pig is a common symbol of wealth, especially in Kentucky, where, as we shall read in the third part, a pig could provide sustenance through a long, harsh winter. There is also a belief that since pigs must look forward, they symbolize progress.

So there you have the traditional New Year's dinner: black-eyed peas, hog jowls and cabbage. Not only does each element represent good fortune, it also completes a highly nutritious meal packed with vitamins.

New Year Black-Eyed Peas

Some make Hoppin' John to serve on January 1, but the more common and simple dish is as follows, with a slice of fried hog jowl on the side.

1 pound dried black-eyed peas
1 large piece of salty bacon or ham
2 teaspoons black pepper
2 quarts water

Soak the beans overnight and then drain. Place the beans, bacon and pepper in the water and bring to a boil. Since the bacon is already cured, you should not need much extra salt. Simmer for 2 hours and serve with hog jowl and greens.

MESSES OF GREENS

You've read about the friendly rivalry between those who dunk and those who crumble their corn bread in pot likker, but what exactly is pot likker? It's the broth left over after cooking greens; others may throw it away, but canny Kentuckians know better than to toss the vitamin-filled water down the drain when they can enjoy it with a slice of corn bread. (It's also another example of how even the poorest Kentucky residents historically made use of what was available to stay healthy.) Pot likker reportedly has its origins in slavery. Kitchen slaves would cook greens for their masters and save the liquid, with all its goodness, for their own families.

Both wild and cultivated greens have long formed a part of the Kentucky diet. If you consider that many poor settlers had eaten wild plants in their native

Many Kentucky homes once had a storage cellar where produce and canned goods could be kept. *Dorothea Lange, Library of Congress.*

Scotland and Ireland, it is not unreasonable to see how they did the same after crossing the Cumberland Gap. Kentucky's forests were filled with an edible and nutritious bounty, if you knew where to look and how to prepare what you found. Watercress and dandelion greens can now be found on supermarket shelves and on the menus of upscale restaurants, but Kentuckians relished them long before they were trendy, along with dock, purselane, nettle tops and poke, to name just a few. No matter how poor you might be, a highly nutritious and free meal's worth of greens could be found just by wandering through the woods or fields near your home. Together, these were known as sallet greens, meaning that they must be cooked before being eaten.

Poke sallet is such a favorite in parts of eastern Kentucky that an annual festival celebrates it. A wild perennial that can reach heights of eight feet or more, poke is not easy to grow as a commercial crop, but aficionados gather the wild leaves—the roots and berries are toxic. As one avid poke eater explained to me, the trick to making them edible is to "cook the heck out of them." They are boiled until a scum has gathered across the top of the water. This scum was described as the toxicity or the bite. The scum is removed, and that water is discarded. The greens are then added to fresh water with a touch of baking soda to remove any additional bite, and they are boiled again.

Boonesboro Greens

This recipe has supposedly been handed down through descendants of the original settlers at Boonesboro, although in that case, the inclusion of potatoes would be out of place. The settlers would have made ample use of the plentiful supply of wild greens.

1 meaty smoked ham bone
6 cups water
4 quarts of greens (equal parts of dandelion greens, poke, dock, mustard
    and wild lettuce, along with smaller portions of violet leaves, plantain,
    nettle tops and milkweed shoots)
2 potatoes, diced
salt and pepper to taste

Simmer the ham bone in the water for 1½ hours. Add the greens. Season and simmer for 45 minutes. After 30 minutes, add the diced potatoes. Remove the ham bone from the pot, cut off the meat and return the meat to the pot. Serve the greens with hard-boiled eggs and vinegar, making sure to reserve the pot likker for later use.

By the way, are you a collard greens or a turnip greens person? It seems a rather silly question, but many have written of staunch allegiances with one or the other. John Egerton defined the dividing line as somewhat equivalent to the Mason-Dixon line, with Kentucky falling firmly in the turnip greens realm. Whichever you choose—or perhaps you straddle the fence with mustard greens—they are traditionally cooked with a slab of bacon or ham, boiled until it might seem that there is little left to eat. As a child who grew up loathing cabbage, I was most surprised to discover a hidden love for turnip greens, particularly when served with a sprinkling of apple cider vinegar. Sometimes you just can't beat a mess of greens.

Turnip Greens

Whichever form of greens you prefer, the preparation is often the same. As Mary Harris Frazer made clear in her recipe here, the inclusion of ham or bacon is not optional to a true Kentuckian—it's a must:

> *Remove all hard part, then wash greens in 4 waters and put in cold water to soak ½ an hour. Have in kettle a piece of jowl or fat bacon; cook until almost done, then add the greens and cook 1 hour.*

A plate of fried catfish and hush puppies still has something missing: coleslaw. Cabbage dates back to the Roman era and beyond, and it was introduced to the United States at some point by early colonists. However, it took Dutch and German influences to make it more interesting than just a boiled green.

Although the Romans ate a dish of shredded cabbage with vinegar and spices, the word *coleslaw* is widely believed to have Dutch roots, meaning that the name for the dish may date perhaps to the Middle Ages. It comes from the Dutch *koolsla*, or cabbage salad. Dutch immigrants brought the dish with them when they came to New York (then New Netherland) in the seventeenth century. As the dish's popularity spread among non-Dutch, the name often became distorted into cold slaw, thus also meriting a hot version. It is not unusual to find recipes for both hot and cold slaw in older cookbooks. Once mayonnaise became more widely known and used, it was found to be an excellent addition to this cabbage salad. Now it is a southern staple, available in dressings made with mayonnaise, vinegar, buttermilk or even sorghum.

Another common use for cabbage, one that stems from Kentucky's German and Jewish populations, is sauerkraut (literally "sour cabbage"). Sometimes misattributed to the Dutch, this fermented cabbage was brought over in barrels by the Pennsylvania Dutch (Amish) when they migrated. Some food historians believe that the dish may, in fact, be from China, having eventually made its way to eastern Europe via migrating tribesmen. Sauerkraut is popular throughout many eastern European countries, often with minor regional alterations to the recipe. Incidentally, the Amish also maintain a tradition of eating cabbage or sauerkraut with pork at New Year.

Marion Flexner's Kentucky Coleslaw

1 head green cabbage
1 tablespoon flour
½ teaspoon dry mustard
1 teaspoon salt
1 tablespoon sugar
2 eggs, beaten
¼ cup water
¼ cup apple cider vinegar
1 tablespoon butter
3 tablespoons sour cream

Shred the cabbage finely and put in a bowl of ice water for 20 minutes. Drain and pat dry with a towel. Add the flour, mustard, salt and sugar to the beaten eggs and whisk until smooth. Slowly add the water and vinegar. Pour into a saucepan with the butter and stir constantly over a low heat. Allow to cook until thick. Remove from the heat and beat until the mixture is smooth again. (Lumps are likely to form during the cooking process.) Add the sour cream and cook. Mix with the cabbage.

Kentucky Cabbage Casserole

Casseroles consisting of a vegetable and a condensed soup–based sauce, topped with crackers, are a popular Kentucky side dish. Although this one uses cabbage, broccoli, asparagus and green beans are all common variations.

1 medium head of cabbage, shredded
1 cup chopped celery
1 cup onion, diced
1 can condensed cream of celery soup
½ cup milk
2 tablespoons butter, melted
1 cup cracker crumbs

Cook the cabbage and celery in boiling water for 5 to 7 minutes. Sauté the onion in a skillet. Drain the cooked cabbage and add the softened onion. In a casserole dish, mix the soup and milk together with any seasonings you wish to add. Add the cabbage, celery and onions and stir to combine. Pour the melted butter over the cracker crumbs and then sprinkle the crumbs on top of the cabbage. Bake for 30 minutes at 350° F.

While on the subject of greens, we should not overlook the salad. Many mistakenly believe the salad to be a modern culinary invention; they could not be farther from the truth. Salads, in one form or another, date back to medieval England. Such sallets would have included a mixture of vegetables, herbs, even flowers, dressed in vinegar and oil. The fourteenth-century salad here is not very far from one we might enjoy today. Medieval physicians sometimes warned against eating raw vegetables, especially greens, believing them to bring about ill health; therefore, some salads would have included cooked vegetables.

Medieval English Onion Salad

parsley, chopped
sage
rosemary
thyme
mint
onions, sliced
leeks, sliced into rounds
garlic, minced
olive oil
red wine vinegar
salt

Chop the herbs and mix with the onions, leek and garlic. Dress with oil, vinegar and salt.

Salads containing such ingredients as dandelion greens, spinach and wilted lettuce were especially popular among the early settlers in Kentucky because it was believed they would "thin the blood which had thickened during the winter." While the concept of blood thickening may not be true, the greens did help to prevent two all-too-common ailments: scurvy and rickets.

John B. Bibb was born to Richard and Lucy Booker Bibb in Virginia in 1789. His family moved to Kentucky in 1798, settling first in Fayette County and then making their way farther west, first to Bullitt County and then to Logan County. John studied law once he was old enough. When the War of 1812 broke out, the twenty-three-year-old joined the Fourth Kentucky Volunteer Brigade, one of several Kentucky regiments. After victory at the Battle of the Thames, Bibb was promoted to the rank of major. Following the war, he returned to Logan County, in southwest Kentucky, was admitted to the bar and pursued his legal career. Naturally, that led to politics.

In 1827, he was elected to the Kentucky House of Representatives. This was followed by a term in the state Senate from 1830 to 1834. In the 1840s, John and his wife, Sarah, moved to Frankfort, where they built Gray Gables; the house still stands today but is now known as the Bibb-Burnley House. With a large garden and impressive greenhouses, Bibb was able to indulge in his hobby as an amateur horticulturalist. It was here that he developed a new variety of lettuce, known first as limestone lettuce but later as the Bibb, regarded by many chefs as the finest of all lettuce varieties. Yet the Bibb lettuce was not made commercially available until 1935, some fifty years after his death. Had he not shared some of the seed with friends, it might not have survived at all.

Wilted Lettuce

This local favorite is believed to have been introduced by German immigrants. Pouring hot oil over cold lettuce may seem odd, but the results are surprisingly good.

¼ pound lettuce (Bibb lettuce works very well here)
6 slices of bacon
1 teaspoon sugar
¼ cup vinegar
¼ teaspoon salt
⅛ teaspoon black pepper

Put lettuce into a bowl. Fry the bacon and remove it from the skillet when done. Add the sugar, vinegar, salt, and pepper to the bacon grease and pour over the lettuce. The grease will cause the greens to wilt. After a few minutes, crumble the bacon over the lettuce and serve.

MORE THAN JUST GREENS

Other vegetables grown included tomatoes, beets, carrots, onions and turnips, but there were a few others of note, some cultivated and some wild.

Ramps

Like most of the wild greens mentioned in the previous section, ramps are one of those Kentucky foods that were ignored in traditional cookbooks. Nothing more than peasant food for those mountain folk, or slaves—hardly something to be found on the dinner plate of a well-to-do Victorian-era housewife. Yet this member of the leek family was, like so many other wild plants, essential to the survival of many Kentuckian settlers. What's more, in the last few decades there has been a growing interest in all things wild as they relate to food, meaning that ramps now feature on the menus of haute cuisine restaurants as far afield as New York. It seems the area's Native American population knew a thing or two about good, healthy food, because as well as tasting wonderful, ramps contain more vitamin C than an orange and hold a number of germicidal effects. Allegedly, it was from them that the settlers learned about ramps. The gathering and eating of ramps would have been an essential part of spring for many eastern Kentuckians.

They look rather like a green onion, but their taste is much stronger. Some people like to eat them raw, although their garlicky odor may render the eater without fellow human company for several days...unless their friends are also ramp lovers. Commonly fried or boil, ramps make an excellent substitute for onions or garlic in scrambled eggs or with bacon, ham and a traditional breakfast.

Morels

Another delicacy much sought after in Kentucky is the morel. These mushrooms—which Mary Hufford, a Pennsylvania professor of folklore, described as tasting "intensely but ethereally earthy"—are known by a variety of names, including hickory chickens and molly moochers. Every spring, people take to the fields, searching for the precious morel, which has a growing season of just a few weeks. Many people eat them either breaded and fried or cooked in a cream sauce.

Squash

The word *squash* is believed to be derived from a Massachusetts Indian word, *askutasquash*, which means "eaten raw." This implies that the concept of cooking came later—fortunately so, since few today would relish the idea of eating a raw pumpkin. And while squash is technically a fruit, since most people identify or use them as vegetables, they are included in this chapter. Kentucky is home to many squash of both summer and winter varieties, including the pumpkin and the cushaw.

There are three main varieties of squash, and they all originated in South or Central America. The ones that are most commonly used in Kentucky—summer squash (zucchini), pumpkin and cushaw—all come from Mexico. Their seeds were carried north by Native Americans, who found that they grew well in most climates. In Kentucky cooking, one can expect to find the hard-skinned squashes, such as pumpkins and cushaw, in both savory and sweet dishes. As well as the ubiquitous pumpkin pie, they can be used in casseroles, chilies, soups, cakes and much more. But it is the cushaw that many people, even lifelong Kentuckians, may not have heard of. It is used by the Native Americans of the southwestern United States, Louisianans in some Cajun and Creole cooking and here in parts of Kentucky. Those who have tried it seem to either love it or hate it. Eliza Leslie found the cushaw "much finer than the summer squash." As one cushaw fan told me, "They make great pies. You mix 'em with a whole heap of sugar and bake 'em into a pie. You can't really taste it because of all the sugar, but yep, them cushaws are good." Uncertain whether this counts as a ringing endorsement, I also point you to the advice given in one of the Shaker cookbooks:

> If your family likes squash, consider this economical variety too-often bypassed. If your family dislikes squash, introduce it as "cushaw."

Baked Cushaw Casserole

2 cups cooked cushaw
1 cup sugar
½ cup butter
1 teaspoon vanilla extract
⅓ cup milk
2 eggs
½ cup brown sugar
1 tablespoon cinnamon
chopped pecans

Combine the cushaw, sugar, butter, vanilla, milk and eggs. Place in a casserole dish. Sprinkle brown sugar, cinnamon and pecans on top. Bake at 350° F for 35 minutes.

Louisville celebrated its first Christmas in 1778, and pumpkin pie was on the menu. Much as the image of pumpkin pie is now inseparable from the United States, it seems to have started life in France. One possibility is that Spanish explorers took seeds back with them, and they made their way through Europe. A recipe for "Tourte de Pompion" (as pumpkin was then known in France) can be found in a seventeenth-century French cookbook; it does not differ widely from modern recipes, except for the lack of spices. This was remedied in a 1685 English recipe that in addition to cinnamon, nutmeg and cloves features thyme, rosemary, apples, currants and wine. "Pompkin" made its way back across the Atlantic to the colonies, where it eventually became "pumpkin." Although early colonists did not have ovens in which a true pie could be cooked, by the time the first proper American cookbook, *American Cookery, or The Art of Dressing…*, was published by Amelia Simmons in 1796, pumpkin pudding baked in a dough crust merited two separate recipes, the second of which noted:

No. 2. One quart of milk, 1 pint pompkin, 4 eggs, molasses, allspice and ginger in a crust, bake 1 hour.

Corn, beans and greens are often held in such high regard in the South that the role of one particular vegetable is ignored or misunderstood. Just as it became a mainstay of the diet in the British Isles once introduced from the Americas, so the humble potato was a staple for many rural Kentuckians. Nutritious and versatile, the potato could be grown on a small plot of land but with a high yield. Although it was rather hard work to plant and harvest, the "tater" crop could last well through the winter when stored in a dry environment.

Potatoes originated in the Andes of Peru and Chile in South America, but we know that Spanish explorers knew of them by the mid-sixteenth century. Several conquistadors wrote of them, and in 1565 Gonzalo Jiménez de Quesada introduced the potato to the Spanish court. He had sailed to the New World hoping to find gold but returned with the tuber—one might argue a much richer find. It was soon noted that potatoes, assumed to be a sort of truffle, prevented scurvy during long months at sea.

One of the first recorded arrivals of the potato in England was in 1597, when London surgeon, author and gardener John Gerard received some roots for his rare plant collection. Upon planting, Gerard found that he was able to grow the Virginia potato (so named to distinguish it as different to the sweet potato) quite successfully. However, given the potato's relationship to the poisonous nightshade family, most people were suspicious of it. Indeed, a decade before Gerard grew some, Sir Walter Raleigh returned from America with the vegetable and planted it on his Irish estate. It is said that he introduced them to Queen Elizabeth I, but since the cooks were unaccustomed to cooking this strange new plant, they instead served the roots and leaves, making everyone ill. As a result, the potato is believed to have been banned at the Royal Court. Further legend has it that Raleigh then ordered that the plant be removed from his estate. While doing so, the servants decided to try the tuber that they found beneath the soil and realized that it was quite tasty—thus the Irish love affair with the potato began.

In 1659, the Royal Society was founded in England with the goal of bringing together eminent scientists to better humanity. The society's earliest focus was on agriculture, looking at what crops could be grown for maximum profit and maximum benefit for the peasant masses. The planting of orchards was encouraged, as was the nationwide planting of potatoes. Having seen how quickly potatoes had been adopted in neighboring Ireland, where they had gone a long way in alleviating starvation, society members saw the potential for England. Interestingly, they stressed the ability to make potatoes into flour, which could, in turn, be used for breads. Several treatises were written on the planting and growth of the potato. However, the audience was small. Even one hundred years later, potatoes would be found only in a few regions of the country.

Across the channel in Ireland, potatoes had been adopted after English landlords burned the corn fields and drove away the cattle in their bid to redistribute Irish land. Since potatoes grew underground, they were unharmed by whatever took place above ground. With milk and corn gone—the two food staples—the potato proved an adequate replacement. And if you didn't have water to boil them in? Just throw them in the ashes of the fire, and they would bake. With all other foods and produce sent to England under the orders of Charles II, the Irish were left to subsist on potatoes. A little less than two hundred years later, when famine and blight hit Ireland, the potato would prove to be both a blessing and a curse. Even during the harshest periods of the famine, the potato continued to be the staple food whenever possible, and a number of creative dishes were born, including Colcannon and Boxty. On the other hand, the knowledge of how to forage for wild greens and even how to fish the rich waters around the coast had been lost, neglected for generations. Foodways that had once fed their ancestors were now out of reach and foreign, and thus death from starvation was widespread.

Although from South America, the potato was introduced to North America by way of European immigrants. Scotch-Irish settlers began planting them in New Hampshire in the early eighteenth century, and their popularity grew from that point on. A little more than a century later, missionaries took them to what is now Idaho, now widely regarded as the Potato State. Yet many continued to regard the potato as unfit for human consumption and suitable only for hogs, even as late as the 1850s, while the Irish Potato Famine was underway across the Atlantic. Others thought them poisonous—if not the potato itself then at least the water in which it was cooked. In her *Directions for Cookery*, Miss Eliza Leslie cautioned:

> *Potatoes, if boiled in the soup, are thought by some to render it unwholesome, from the opinion that the water in which potatoes have been cooked is almost a poison. As potatoes are a part of every dinner, it is very easy to take a few out of the pot in which they have been boiled by themselves, and to cut them up and add them to the soup just before it goes to the table.*

Eventually, of course, people realized that perhaps the potato was worth some consideration. Once they accepted the concept that it was not poisonous and was indeed rather edible, it became the popular tater that we know and love.

Potato Snow

Many of the recipes for the preparation of potatoes contained in early cookbooks are easily recognizable to the modern cook, but this one, from Lettice Bryan's *The Kentucky Housewife*, stood out as being a little different:

Very old potatoes or very young ones are not fit for snow, the former being heavy and sodden, while preparing the latter for snow renders them insipid. Select large white, full grown potatoes, which are quite dry and farinaceous. Wash them clean, put them in a kettle with enough cold water to cover them little over an inch, as when boiled into little water, they will not be so white. Boil them rather briskly till done, which you may tell by trying them with a fork, or by taking one out, and mashing it. Then turn off the remaining water immediately, set the kettle by the fire for a few minutes, throwing over it a folded napkin or flannel, to absorb the superfluous moisture; after which peel them, rub them through a coarse wire sieve, letting the snow fall into a dish, forming a pyramidal heap: do not disturb it in any way, but sent it immediately to table with salt, pepper and a boat of drawn butter, to be handed round with it to the company, that they may season it to suit their own tastes. Potato snow is very pretty when properly made, but if sent to the table without the seasonings, it is quite an insipid dish.

Potato Salad

It is probably safe to say that for every cook in Kentucky, there is a slightly different recipe for potato salad. Whether or not to add mustard, bacon, egg or vinegar…some might consider them personal preferences, while others would consider them unbreakable rules of potato salad. Even most cookbooks offer more than one variation. Frazer provided one recipe with eggs, celery, mustard and walnuts and another with cayenne pepper, capers and mayonnaise. The Shakers make a German potato salad with bacon and vinegar, advising that a good German cook will know to "have the potatoes cold and the bacon limp." The recipe shared here is just one of many.

6 potatoes, peeled	1 cup mayonnaise
1 onion, chopped	½ cup buttermilk
2 stalks celery, finely chopped	2 tablespoons sugar
4 pickles, chopped	2 tablespoons apple cider vinegar
2 hard-boiled eggs, chopped	salt and paprika to taste

Boil the potatoes. When they are cooled, chop them. Place in a bowl with the onion, celery, pickles and hard-boiled eggs. Combine mayonnaise, buttermilk, sugar and vinegar. Add salt and paprika to taste. Pour over the vegetables and blend well.

APPLES: CUSTARD, CRAB AND CULTIVATED

Every fall, a few select stores and farmers' markets begin displaying a rather odd-looking fruit that is quickly snatched up by those in the know. This same fruit was said to have sustained explorers Lewis and Clark on some parts of their journey into the western wilderness. But you have to be quick—their season is short, and they do not transport well. Some people loathe them, but for those who love them, this short window of opportunity is a culinary delight. The fruit in question is the pawpaw.

Not to be confused with the tropical papaya, the American pawpaw is also known as the custard apple. It can range in size from barely the size of an apple to more than six inches long, and it is one of the largest native fruits in the United States. (I will shy from claiming, as some do, that it is the largest, because that may unleash indignation from pumpkin enthusiasts!) Green on the outside, there is little exterior indication of ripeness. Inside, the flesh ranges in color from a delicate cream to a vivid orange.

Their natural habitat actually extends a fair distance through the eastern half of the continent, but because of their difficulty to cultivate and transport, as well as their short season, few people know of them unless they grew up picking wild pawpaws in nearby woods. Many native Kentuckians will talk eagerly of traipsing through local woods in search of the precious fruit. Some will cook with them, and others will freeze the pulp, but one of the favorite ways to eat them is to simply scoop out the creamy-textured flesh with a spoon, much like a custard.

But what do they taste like? Their flavor can vary as much as their color, but it is a subtle combination of flavors: hints of peach and banana, a touch of pineapple or mango and perhaps some vanilla. It is both light and complex.

Pawpaw Pie

Cooking with pawpaws can be difficult because they contain similar enzymes to pineapple, meaning that they may not set into a pie or tart with gelatin. Using agar agar instead should help.

½ cup brown sugar
2 teaspoons agar agar
⅔ cup milk
3 eggs, separated
1 cup pawpaw pulp
¼ cup sugar
1 9-inch cracker-crumb pie base

Over a low heat, combine the brown sugar and agar agar. Add the milk and the egg yolks. Stir well and increase the heat to bring the mixture to a boil. Once the mixture reaches a boil, remove the pan from the heat and stir in the pawpaw pulp. Leave to cool in the refrigerator. As it cools, the mixture will start to set. Beat the egg whites until they stand in soft peaks. Add the sugar to the egg whites and beat until stiff. Carefully fold the egg whites and pawpaw mix together. Spoon into the crumb base and chill until the pie filling has set. If you like, you can top with whipped cream before serving.

Pawpaw Jam

6 cups pawpaw puree
4 cups sugar
1 package pectin

Simmer the puree and slowly add the sugar. When all the sugar is added and stirred in, simmer for another 8 minutes. Add the pectin and then bring the mixture to a rolling boil. Turn off the heat. Place in jars and seal in a water bath.

Apples

Another introduction from the Old World, apples have become a staple not just of Kentucky but also of much of the nation. By the end of the nineteenth century, the United States Department of Agriculture listed some eight thousand varieties of apples. With names like Northern Spy, Maiden's Blush and Winter Banana, there were varieties suited to every season and every use, from eating raw to cooking in pies or making cider. Many of these varieties have now died out, and the most popular variety without a doubt is the Golden Delicious, which writers John and Karen Hess deride as having "hardly any taste at all." They lament, "One might as well follow the directions on a carton of Ritz Crackers and make a 'Mock Apple Pie: no apples needed!' It is indeed only a short step from Delicious to no apple at all." Fortunately, in Kentucky, there are many local apple orchards, all of which celebrate the fall apple harvest with festivals, fried apple pies, cider and such alternatives to the Delicious as the Jonathan, McIntosh, Goldrush and the Stayman Winesap.

When the first settlers arrived in the United States and later in Kentucky, they found crab apples, the only type native to the continent—not that these were without their uses. Daniel Drake remembered of Kentucky's infancy:

> Crab apples were gathered after they had been exposed to the mellowing influences of a few white frosts. This tree, the color, form and odor of whose flowers are equally beautiful and delicious, was always found solitary (while the pawpaw formed groves or patches). It was our great resource for preserves throughout the year—and certainly no cultivated fruit is better.

The first attempts to grow English apple trees in the New World failed to produce fruit because of the absence of honeybees. These, too, were imported from Europe, and orchards flourished. John Chapman (aka Johnny Appleseed) would later spend much of his lifetime wandering the frontier states of the Midwest, planting apple trees wherever he went.

The first white families to arrive in Kentucky found that the Native Americans had planted some peach trees, the fruit having been introduced by the Spanish farther south a few centuries earlier. Peaches became a useful crop, providing butters, jams and brandy. Eventually, though, the cultivated apple replaced them. Apples had better growing seasons and could be stored for longer. Some would keep their apples in the root cellar; others would have large storage chests lined with sawdust to keep the fruit dry and protect them against the frost. When stored in this manner, they could last the entire winter and still be good when eaten in the spring. Daniel Drake wrote that the apples "wouldn't freeze. They'd keep bushels and bushels of apples all winter. Fresh apples. And they'd be so crispy and

Men picking fruit at one of Kentucky's many apple orchards, dated 1914. *Louis Edward Nollau Nitrate Photographic Print Collection, University of Kentucky.*

juicy. They wouldn't freeze because you had them in that insulated box. Apples can take chill and cold."

He went on to describe the communal apple harvest and cooperative apples peelings, where friends would gather to prepare the apples for winter. Some were peeled and dried for later use, others were cooked into apple butter or pie filling and still more would be pressed into cider. Originally, this would have been a hard cider, but as the temperance movement grew in influence, it became the unfermented type found today. Those that were dried were sometimes left to dry in the sun, a method that required no extra equipment. Some people preferred to sulfur them, exposing them to sulfur smoke to kill any bacteria, bleaching them white in the process.

Apple Butter (from the Kentucky Receipt Book)

Frazer offered two recipes for apple butter, one of which is a mere two sentences: "For 1 gallon of apples, 1½ pounds of sugar. Flavor with allspice." For those seeking a little more detail, she also provided the following:

> One peck of apples, 2 gallons reduced cider, cinnamon, and nutmeg. Use new cider, and boil until reduced ½. It must be boiled the day before it

is needed. Pare, core and quarter the apples, put in porcelain kettle as many at a time as the cider will moisten, add until all are cooked. Stir constantly and beat apples to a pulp, as fast as they soften. When reduced to a thick paste, add some brown sugar and spices. Boil a few minutes longer. Then put in jars. Water may be substituted for cider, and in that case, use more sugar.

Fried Apples

Fried apples are a popular side dish at breakfast or dinner. Although best suited to go with pork or ham, I know many Kentuckians who will happily eat them with anything. Some like the apples to remain fairly firm, while others prefer a softer finished product. This will vary according to cooking time and the variety of apple used.

6 apples
4 tablespoons bacon grease
⅓ cup sugar

Peel, core and slice the apples. Heat the bacon grease and fry the apple slices until they are golden brown, adding a little water if necessary. Add the sugar and continue cooking until the apples are the consistency you prefer.

PART III

MEAT AND FISH

HIGH ON THE HOG

May you always eat high on the hog.
—*Kentucky saying*

If beans and corn are two Kentucky staples, pork is surely the third part of the commonwealth's culinary trinity. Whether it be the small piece of bacon added to the shucky beans or the barbecued hog roast reserved for special occasions, pork is the meat that forms the basis of many Kentucky meals. Rick McDaniel has called it "the most important meat in the South." There was a time when no self-respecting Kentucky cook was without a jar of bacon grease next to the stove, collected from cooking previous dinners and carefully saved for future use. This practice is making a comeback among many cooks as natural fats regain favor. Indeed, ownership of a hog was an asset to any family. Popular legend still tells that the famous Hatfield-McCoy feud began with a court battle over ownership of a pig (despite historical evidence that land rights were also an important factor).

Archaeological evidence shows that pigs roamed the wilds of what is now Europe and Asia as much as 40 million years ago. The Chinese were the first to domesticate them, followed by the Europeans in roughly 1500 BC. Pigs first arrived on the American continent with Columbus in 1493, reputedly at the insistence of Queen Isabella. In 1539, Hernando de Soto landed in Florida with thirteen porcine companions; within three years, his swine herd was an estimated seven hundred strong. Pork was a staple in the Spanish Catholic diet, largely since it served to prove one's identity as neither Jew nor Muslim—both religions had been expected to convert or leave Spain in events that prefigured the Spanish Inquisition. The desire to rout out non-Catholics came with the Spaniards to the New World. Pigs were steadily introduced to other parts of the country with Cortez, Sir Walter Raleigh and English settlers in New England, and as some escaped, a population of wild pigs grew. Some even offer protection from the wild pigs as the reason for the construction of the original wall on what is now Wall Street in New York; in 1653, Dutch director general Peter Stuyvesant wrote of the damage done by foraging pigs. The wall may have held back some of the swine, but visitors to New York continued to write of pigs roaming free, even in the nicer neighborhoods, well into the nineteenth century. Indeed, when Kentuckian Mary Todd Lincoln first visited Washington, D.C., after her husband's election to the U.S. House of Representatives, she was taken aback to see pigs wandering freely in the unpaved streets. Such sights were to be expected in Lexington, but surely not in the nation's capital.

No animal was better suited to the rough conditions of the Appalachian frontier than the hog. As more immigrants crossed the Cumberland Gap, they soon realized that the land was ill-suited for the sheep and cattle of Scotland and Ireland. Where would they graze? But pigs could run wild and survive on a diet of just about anything, and when it was time, virtually every part of them had a use in the kitchen. The predilection for pork products did not escape the notice of those who visited the state. In 1806, Irish writer Thomas Ashe passed through. He later complained about the Kentucky diet:

> *The Kentuckyan* [sic] *ate nothing but bacon, which indeed is the favorite diet of all the inhabitants of the State, and drank nothing but whiskey… They eat salt meat three times a day, seldom or never have any vegetable, and drink ardent spirits from morning till night! The truth is, their stomachs are depraved.*

Before you fret about the well-being of the notoriously fussy Mr. Ashe during his visit, fear not, for he did eventually find some good eating. After agreeing to dinner with a woman and her family because he pitied her, he ate for dinner "[a] large piece of salt bacon, a dish of homslie [hominy] and a tureen of squirrel broth. I dined entirely on the last dish, which I found incomparably good, and the meat equal to delicate chicken."

In *Dishes and Beverages of the Old South*, Martha McCulloch-Williams went into great detail describing the butchering of hogs, noting that "hog-killing was a festival as joyous as Christmas—and little less sacred." The process was most meticulous. First, the right hog must be selected; Mary Randolph believed hogs to be "in the highest perfections" when between two and a half and four years old and when fed on corn for at least six weeks before killing. The hog was killed using an axe to sever the head, and then chops were made through the ribs and joints. The backbone was removed and chopped into smaller pieces; these would be used to make either a stew or a pie so tasty it could apparently rival any chicken pie. Hams and shoulders would be cut and put to one side for smoking, while the sides were either cut into bacon strips or left as larger bacon joints. The head was also butchered, with each part providing a meal of some sort. Sometimes it was boiled with cabbage and beans. Alternatively, it was used with the feet to make headcheese (souse). McCulloch-Williams noted that the feet were also wonderful when boiled, dredged in cornmeal and fried. The oil that was extracted from the feet would be used to dress leather. Brains would be fried or pickled, and the jowls were eaten with black-eyed peas and boiled cabbage on New Year's Day to bring good luck for the coming year (a tradition that continues to this day).

With the fat rendered into lard and any remaining scraps turned into sausage, that left the work of preserving the meat and curing the hams, which, as it happens, is taken mighty seriously in Kentucky.

Country Ham

The Kentucky country ham has long been a source of great pride to those who prepare it, as well as a source of great enjoyment to those privileged to eat it. Cured over hickory fires and left to season in smokehouses for a year or more, a proper country ham is a valuable and a much-loved commodity. Alan Deutschman called it "a product of peasant genius and simplicity." Peasant genius perhaps, but one that now commands quite a price; the 2009 Kentucky State Fair Grand Champion Ham, produced by Scott Hams in Greenville, eventually sold for $1.3 million. The following year, Broadbent's won the ribbon; that ham sold for $1.6

NATIONAL CHAMPION COUNTRY HAM 2008

GRAND CHAMPION KY STATE FAIR 2007

1st PLACE KY STATE FAIR 2006

1st PLACE KY STATE FAIR 2005

1st PLACE KY STATE FAIR 2004

1st PLACE at KY STATE FAIR 2003

RESERVE GRAND CHAMPION NATIONAL CURED MEAT SHOW 2003

1st PLACE at KY STATE FAIR 2002

GRAND CHAMPION NATIONAL CURED MEAT SHOW 2002

RESERVE GRAND CHAMPION NATIONAL CURED MEAT SHOW 2001

1st PLACE at KY STATE FAIR 2001

RESERVE GRAND CHAMPION NATIONAL CURED MEAT SHOW 99

Country ham is a source of pride, as this list of accolades won by Scott Hams in Greenville demonstrates.

million, just under $100,000 per pound! (The proceeds from these sales go to charity.) Those who sell Kentucky hams today pride themselves on continuing a tradition that has been practiced for generations. Father's Country Hams in Bremen uses curing techniques that have been in the family since 1840.

Once upon a time, families made their own hams, a useful means of preserving some of the precious hog for use at a later date. The Kentucky climate is ideal for the preparation of these hams. The best ham requires a climate with about forty days of forty-degree temperatures; many other locations are too cold or too hot. As refrigeration became more readily available, even in poorer rural areas, and as more women worked outside the home, there was less inclination and less need to go through the time-consuming process of salting and hanging hams. However, the taste for country ham was not lost. As a result, some farms began commercial country ham enterprises.

Hams are typically dry-cured, which means that they are first rubbed thoroughly with salt. Salt curing eventually gave way to so-called sugar curing, which simply meant that sugar was included with the salt, the latter still being the principal ingredient. John and Anne van Willigen gave one recipe for a sugar cure: "12 quarts of salt, 3 pounds of sugar, 1 pound of black pepper, and a scant teaspoon of saltpeter to cure 500 pounds of meat." Whichever curing method is used, the curing mixture is rubbed onto the meat to form a layer of at least one inch in thickness. Then they are placed in more salt for a specific period (up to two months) in carefully controlled temperatures. Often they would be kept in a large, deep box completely filled with salt so that the joints of pork were completely encased.

After curing, the hams are washed and hung to dry. At this stage, they may have some more salt or sugar rubbed into them. The hams are often smoked over fresh hickory wood before being hung to age. During this time, they often develop white specks of mold on the exterior, something that can be off-putting to the country ham novice, but they are easily rinsed away. Rufus Jarman noted that true lovers of country ham "would admire that growth of mold as a mark of age and distinction, like the beard of a prophet."

Among Kentucky's commercial country ham producers, Scott Hams rubs its hams with salt and brown sugar and then ages them for a year—and no more. Beyond two years, the ham runs the risk of becoming too dry or of attracting mites. Likewise, Father's Country Hams admits to using hickory smoke, sugar and salt. Beyond that, each family's individual technique and recipe are closely guarded secrets. Although hams are also produced in surrounding states, particularly Virginia, connoisseurs of the Kentucky ham believe it to be far superior in taste. Marion Flexner described the flavor as "richer, more nut-like and delicate" and suspected that it might be a result of the local hickory wood.

During the aging process, a ham loses much of its weight in water, and so water must be added when cooking. Some people like to boil a whole ham, while others fry slices as they need it and enjoy it with red eye gravy.

Much has been made of so-called illegal country ham. Calvin Trillin wrote that "the most authentic country hams were illegal" and how the country ham people eat at home must be bought at a supermarket. Obviously, this conjures up bootlegger-style images of old jalopies racing toward the county line, the law in hot pursuit, hams bouncing around on the back seat. The reality is much less exciting, as several country ham makers explained. The U.S. Department of Agriculture has certain regulations in place to protect the consumer by guaranteeing that any product sold as country ham meets certain specifications with regards to process and hygiene. The downside of this is that technically, anyone who meets these regulations can sell "country ham" or a product labeled as such, even if it has been aged for a mere forty-two days, far less than the six months to two years that any reputable country ham has been aged. On the other hand, many ham producers in western Kentucky say that the regulations did not demand anything further than what they were already doing. What's more, the law does not apply to individuals making food for their own consumption, so any farmer can continue to make and eat his own country hams. He just can't sell them across state lines or via mail order. Making it and eating it is not illegal; making it commercially available is. And if you want to be sure that you are eating proper country ham, produced using the traditional methods and aged appropriately, buy it from the source rather than the supermarket. As John Egerton wrote, "[T]hey are the true artists, the last of the masters."

Fried Country Ham

Pre-sliced country ham can be readily found, but if using a whole ham, cut slices that are about a quarter inch in thickness. Put in a skillet with enough water to nearly cover the ham slices. Cover the skillet and simmer for about half an hour until tender, turning the ham occasionally. Note that you want the water to simmer, not boil.

Red Eye Gravy

Although this gravy is often thought of as containing coffee, food writer John Egerton noted that "if the ham is real ham, coffee won't be necessary." Once you have fried your slices of ham, add a cup or so of water to the ham drippings and simmer for a few minutes.

Kentucky Ham Bone Soup

1 ham hock
3 quarts water
1 quart tomatoes
½ teaspoon black pepper

3 onions, chopped
4 potatoes, diced
1 cabbage, shredded

Boil the ham in the water with the tomatoes, pepper and 1 of the onions. Simmer for 2 hours. Add the potatoes, cabbage and the remaining onions and simmer for 2 more hours. Skim off the fat and add salt if needed. Serve with corn bread.

Kentucky Oysters

The eagle-eyed reader might have noticed one part of the hog missing from the butchering instructions. No doubt certain organs remained too delicate for southern women to mention, even those accustomed to the annual hog-killing ritual. Some parts of the country have lamb fries; hog-killing time had Kentucky oysters. According to Mark Kurlansky's research, these were a popular seasonal treat for African Americans, who might happen to be helping with the preparation of the hog for winter: "Placed in cans for commercial use, this part of the hog is in season according to the same tradition as the salt water bivalve from which it gets its name." The "oysters" could be prepared in one of two ways: boiled or parboiled, breaded and fried. However they were cooked, they should be served with slaw and corn bread.

BURGOO AND BARBECUE

Who, excepting Kentuckians and their favored Southern Friends and kinsmen, has ever really known the bliss of genuine burgoo?
—Washington Post, 1906

The state of Minnesota has booya, commonly believed to be derived from the French word *bouillabaisse*, a stew prepared on a grand scale for hundreds of people or more. It is cooked over several days in giant kettles and contains a variety of meats and vegetables.

Several southern states compete for the title of the home of Brunswick stew, a thick, meaty stew believed to have originated in Germany. It, too, is cooked slowly in large kettles and contains a combination of meats and vegetables. Different regions have slightly different versions of it. Here in Kentucky, we have burgoo. And as the *Washington Post* so rightly noted, genuine burgoo is bliss.

Burgoo's origins are much debated. For one thing, there's the name. Where does it come from? What does it mean? According to the *Dictionary of American Food and Drink*, burgoo was an oatmeal porridge eaten by British sailors in the mid-eighteenth century, the name of which came from the Middle Eastern word *burghul* (bulghur wheat). One cannot help but wonder how oatmeal porridge developed into the meaty vegetable stew of today.

Making burgoo at a Democratic barbecue in Winchester, Kentucky, September 1916.
Postcard Collection at the University of Kentucky.

Others claim that the name is a bastardization of some other phrase, perhaps bird stew, barbecue or even the French *ragout*. While I admit that these sound off to my tongue, language has been known to make strange leaps. Gerald Alvey speculated that the term is a shortening of "barbecue goo," referring to the soupy leftovers from making barbecue; given that burgoo and barbecue are centered on the same part of Kentucky, the explanation certainly seems plausible.

Burgoo gained a permanent place in Kentucky history thanks to Gus Jaubert. Born in 1838 and a soldier in the Confederate army, Jaubert is credited by some as having invented the dish, while others say that he simply elevated it to a new status. It is said that he cooked thousands of gallons of the stew for Colonel John Hunt Morgan and his raiders. There are those who claim that it contained blackbirds and that the name burgoo came from Jaubert's inability to pronounce "blackbird stew." However, it should be noted that although of French descent, the cook was born and raised in the United States and therefore unlikely to have had an accent. Later in life, he dismissed the blackbird story. After the war, Jaubert opened a restaurant in Lexington but was often called on to prepare his burgoo for large gatherings. In 1895, he cooked for thousands of Union Civil War veterans in Louisville, serving an estimated six thousand gallons at this one event. Upon Jaubert's death in 1920, a man by the name of James

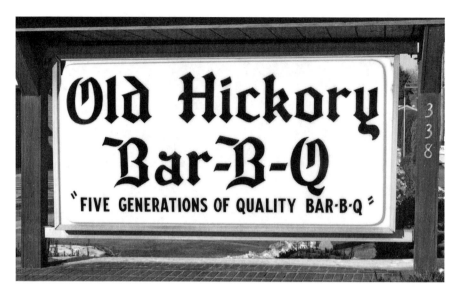

Old Hickory in Owensboro is famous for its burgoo and barbecue.

T. Looney supposedly inherited Jaubert's prized kettle. So famous was Looney as the "Burgoo King" that a horse was named after him and went on to win the 1932 Kentucky Derby.

What's in burgoo? If you ask a dozen people, you'll get a dozen different answers. There is no one recipe, and there are no strict rules to making burgoo. That doesn't mean you won't recognize it when you see it. Some attempts are little more than a beef and potato soup; this is not burgoo. Proper burgoo typically contains more than one meat. Some maintain that in days gone by, this would have been whatever meat could be found—squirrel, deer, pork, rabbit and so on. Old Hickory BBQ in Owensboro uses mutton, pork and chicken in its burgoo. Vegetables may include corn, potatoes and tomatoes. Marion Flexner recalled that Tandy Ellis, who learned to make burgoo from Gus Jaubert himself, took exception to her including cabbage, as leafy greens have no place in burgoo. As for spices, every cook has his or her own selection. Old Hickory's burgoo has a slight sweetness and a tang, which it attributes to a secret ingredient. It should be cooked for a long time, over a hickory fire, so that the meats and other ingredients break down and meld into a thick stew.

In the past, burgoo was served at political rallies and fundraisers. Now you can find it primarily in western Kentucky. Even if burgoo's name does not come from barbecue, the two dishes go together, with Owensboro as their home. Owensboro in Daviess County is at the heart of burgoo country. It is also the self-proclaimed "Bar-B-Q Capital of the World" and home to the International Bar-B-Q Festival, an annual event that brings some sixty thousand or more visitors to the city. An estimated 1,500 gallons of burgoo are served during the course of the festival. There is also an annual festival devoted solely to burgoo, held in Anderson County.

Burgoo

The following recipe is from J.M. Foster, a noted Lexington burgoo cook:

A two pound foreshank soup bone, a two pound pork shank, a breast of lamb and a fat hen; three large onions, three large potatoes, three raw carrots, four large tomatoes, or two medium-sized cans, four ears of green corn, or two cans, two pods of red pepper, two green peppers, half a pint of butter beans, a small bunch of parsley. Cook meat thoroughly, remove from liquor, pour cook water over it in a pan and strip from bones. Chop your meat in an old fashioned chopping bowl. Chop up your vegetables, put meat and vegetables together with water poured over meat, back into the soup kettle and cook till mixture is thick. Four teaspoonfuls of Worcestershire sauce added ten minutes off gives the burgoo tang.

Tandy Ellis's Burgoo Recipe

This version serves anywhere from eight (Ellis's estimate) to twenty (Flexner's).

2 pounds beef from the shank, including the bone
½ pound lamb
1 chicken
4 quarts of water
salt and black pepper
1 pod of red pepper or more to taste
2 cups diced potatoes
2 cups onion, diced

2 cups fresh butterbeans
3 carrots, diced
2 green peppers, diced and with the seeds removed
3 cups corn, cut from the cob
2 cups okra
12 tomatoes
1 clove garlic
1 cup parsley, minced

Put the beef, lamb and dismembered chicken in a soup kettle with the water, salt, black and red pepper. Allow the water to come to a hard boil. Then reduce the heat, cover and simmer for 2 hours. Add the potatoes, onions and, at intervals of about ten minutes, the butterbeans, carrots and green peppers. Add the corn and simmer for two hours, until the mixture is very thick. Add more water if necessary. Add okra, tomatoes and garlic and simmer for a further 1½ hours. Stir the parsley in after removing the pot from the heat. Serve with corn bread.

Barbecue will mean something different based on where you grew up. Everyone will agree that traditional barbecue is cooked long and slow over hot coals or wood, but the seasonings and the type of meat will differ. Residents of Memphis will think of ribs, either with a dry rub or a wet-basted sauce. For Texans, barbecue is often beef cooked over mesquite, but in Carolina, you'll find pulled pork and hickory wood. Meanwhile, in Kansas City, cooks use a dry rub and serve the sauce as a side at the table. Ask about Kentucky barbecue, and you'll be told about mutton in a vinegar-based sauce.

In truth, Kentucky barbecue is much more varied, so much so that Wes Berry devoted an entire book to the types of barbecue to be found across the state. He identified variations so regional that they can be defined by county. But since mutton remains the most commonly thought-of Kentucky style, let's begin with that.

In 1775, Colonel Richard Callaway (often incorrectly cited as Richard Callow) traveled across the Cumberland Gap with Daniel Boone and helped to settle Boonesboro. He brought with him several sheep, and many believe that this is the reason burgoo and barbecue both contain lamb, or mutton. However, if this were the case, surely there would be more lamb in basic Kentucky cooking as opposed to pork. As previously mentioned, the mountains of Appalachia were ill-suited to grazing animals, but in western and central parts of the state, flatter pastureland provided ample opportunity for the raising of sheep. The statesman Henry Clay raised Merinos at Ashland, his estate in Lexington, and Cassius Clay raised Southdowns at his White Hall home in Madison County. Flocks thrived on bluegrass and worked well in rotation with tobacco crops. By 1942, Kentucky had more sheep per square mile than any other state east of the Mississippi with 1.4 million head. That number started to decline soon thereafter. Sheep were regarded as more valuable for their wool than for their meat, and as synthetic fabrics were developed, demand dropped, although there has been a renewed interest in the last decade or so.

It was in the Daviess County area that sheep continued as a food source, and that seems to have been largely due to the area's Catholic population.

Left: The Hot Brown was created to satisfy the hunger of 1920s partygoers. *The Brown Hotel.*

Below: Apple stack cake is best when made over several days, allowing the moisture of the apples to penetrate each layer.

Shaker lemon pie uses whole lemons sliced paper thin and placed in a bowl of sugar to macerate overnight.

Barbecued mutton and burgoo are meaty staples in the Owensboro area.

Left: Kentucky is home to a wide variety of wild greens, all of which satisfy diners today as they did in pioneer times. *Maureen C. Berry.*

Below: The Poor Boy contains two beef patties, cheese, onion, lettuce, tomato, pickle, mustard and the Parkette's special sauce. *The Parkette.*

Left: Buffalo Trace distillery was one of the few allowed to continue producing bourbon during Prohibition. *Buffalo Trace Distillery.*

Right: Inspired by European ginger ales, G.L. Wainscott created Ale-8-One in Winchester, Kentucky. *Ale-8-One.*

Left: Canning and preserving continue to be popular activities in the Kentucky kitchen each fall. *Maureen C. Berry.*

Below: Pumpkin, squash and cushaw all lend themselves to both sweet and savory dishes.

The leftovers from frying sausage make excellent gravy, the perfect accompaniment to biscuits.

Cornmeal cakes are a filling and traditional breakfast. *Beaumont Inn.*

Left: Lima beans and a multitude of heirloom variety beans are part of a conservation project in Appalachia. *Maureen C. Berry.*

Below: Fried chicken, mashed potatoes, gravy and green beans—the quintessential Kentucky dinner.

The chocolate and nut goodness of Derby Pie® is a favorite at many Derby Day parties. *Kern's Kitchens.*

Hog jowls and black-eyed peas are eaten on New Year's Day to bring good luck in the coming year.

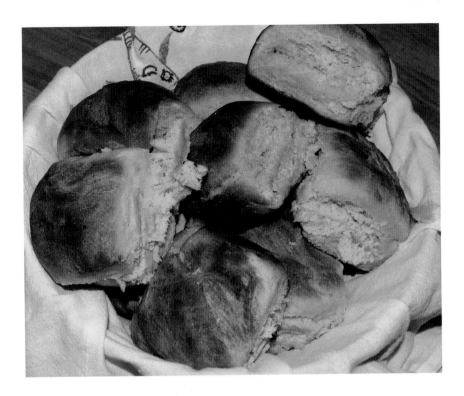

Above: You can expect to find corn bread, biscuits or yeast rolls with most Kentucky meals…or a combination of all three.

Left: Country hams age between six months and two years, resulting in a rich, salty taste.

Above: Jam, nuts and caramel frosting all contribute to the Southern Jam Cake.

Left: Traditional Kentucky food lends itself well to adaptations, such as this Thai-style pulled pork and spicy slaw. *Maureen C. Berry.*

Pawpaws have a short season and a "love it or hate it" taste. Fans can't get enough of them.

The use of railways to ship goods may have declined, but banana pudding remains a part of Kentucky foodways.

Stanford's Bluebird Café offers locally sourced meat and produce.

Cherries are just one of the many fruits available at Kentucky orchards to be baked into pies and jams. *Maureen C. Berry.*

Top: Chili buns from Weaver's Pool Hall, topped with mustard and onions, are both simple and sinful.

Left: Chef Anthony Lamas of Louisville's Seviche has created a Tuna Old Fashioned. Inspired by the cocktail, it includes sustainably produced tuna and Bluegrass Soy Sauce. *Ted Tarquinio*.

The Beaumont Inn puts an elegant spin on fried chicken. *Beaumont Inn.*

It may not look fancy, but the secret to Monroe County–style pork shoulder is to eat the bottom slices first, with all their vinegar flavor.

Left: A zucchini potato gratin is an easy way to make the most of fresh, local Kentucky produce.

Below: Kentucky goodness with a French twist in a fresh strawberry galette. *Maureen C. Berry.*

Chef Ouita Michel turns the Hot Brown inside out. *Wallace Station.*

A traditional Kentucky breakfast of eggs, biscuits and more. *Windy Corner Market.*

Barbecuing beef and lamb for a church benefit near Bardstown. *Marion Post Wolcott, Library of Congress.*

As far back as 1834, churches in the area would hold large community fundraiser picnics. Although the reason why mutton should prove so popular is somewhat vague (but probably owing to the number of Welsh settlers who made their homes here in the early 1800s), these events have always served mutton barbecue and burgoo. Enormous kettles of meat would begin cooking early in the day, ready for the hungry parishioners. Every summer, thousands of people still flock to these feasts to enjoy the barbecued mutton for which the area, and indeed the entire state, has become famous. For anyone who still believes that mutton is a dry, tough meat, one trip to Owensboro's barbecue restaurants can put that to rest. Richly flavored, tender mutton is served with the local "dip"—a combination of Worcestershire sauce, sugar and spices. Cooking mutton successfully does require a cook who knows what he or she is doing, however, which is probably why mutton barbecue remains confined to this small corner of Kentucky.

Down south, by the Tennessee state line, you encounter Monroe County–style barbecue. Pork shoulder, sliced thinly, is cooked over hickory coals before being served with a Monroe County dip. The dip in question is similar to that found in Owensboro but with a sinus-opening kick since it contains a

Kentuckians are proud of their variety of barbecue, and rightly so.

The Smokey Pig in Bowling Green offers Monroe County–style pork shoulder.

heavy dose of cayenne pepper in place of Worcestershire sauce. Farther west, you can expect to find meat smoked over hickory, chopped and served on toast with pickles and raw onion, accompanied again by a vinegary cayenne pepper sauce. So popular is barbecue today in the central and western parts of the state that there are several annual festivals to celebrate it. I have even met people who relocated from other states to be closer to their favorite Kentucky barbecue restaurants.

FRIED CHICKEN

For better or for worse, Kentucky will always be associated with one particular food. No matter what country a Kentuckian finds himself or herself in, as soon as they mention their home state, people will nod in recognition: "Ah, fried chicken."

Sadly, whatever impression they have of fried chicken has been colored by their local fast-food outlets. Such greasy, tasteless fare bears little resemblance to the delight of succulent home-cooked chicken, prepared in grandma's cast-iron skillet using a recipe handed down through the generations.

Fried chicken appears in some form or another in many cultures' histories. In the Middle Ages, the English and French cooked (technically braised rather than fried) chicken portions in cream, what we now know of as a fricassee. Historians have reported that long before this, Romans prepared fritter dishes, and the Scots followed in their footsteps, dredging meat in flour and frying. It is no surprise, therefore, that it should have made its way to the New World. Settlers at Jamestown introduced chickens in 1607 or thereabouts, and by the eighteenth century, they were in plentiful supply. Like hogs, chickens were ideally suited to pioneer living in Kentucky; they could root around and eat whatever they might find. But whereas a family might not be able to afford a hog, all but the very poorest could own a few birds. Nevyle Shackelford recalled that chickens and the eggs they provided were "important financial mainstays of the average farm family." Not only did they provide basic foodstuffs for the family, additional eggs could also always be traded with neighbors or at the local store for other essential items.

Slaves in the South were often allowed to raise their own chickens, and records indicate that they fried them in spices and peanut oil, no doubt adapting recipes brought with them from West Africa. This may well be the method that has had the greatest influence on modern fried chicken.

Early recipe books contain recipes for fried chicken, but many resemble a fricassee as opposed to today's dish. However, in *The Virginia Housewife*, Mary Randolph recommended dredging the pieces in flour and frying in boiling lard. She then created a sort of gravy with milk and herbs to be poured over the chicken. This would seem to be the first published version of the fried chicken we know today. Meanwhile, Lettice Bryan battered her chicken before frying in *The Kentucky Housewife*. A similar recipe to Randolph's is featured in the first cookbook written by an African American woman, *What Mrs. Fisher Knows About Southern Cooking*. Once again, the chicken pieces are dipped in flour, salt and pepper before being dropped in hot fat. Some of the remaining fat is mixed with flour and water to create a gravy.

Regardless of this history, fried chicken would come to be associated with one man. And he was not even from Kentucky.

Harland Sanders was born in Henryville, Indiana, in 1890. When Harland was just five, his father died, leaving a young widow and three small children. As his mother struggled to maintain their small farm and seek additional work in nearby factories, Harland, the eldest, took charge of his young siblings and often sought work himself to assist with the household bills. The early years of his adult life were unremarkable. He worked various jobs as a teen before joining the army. Recurrent seasickness meant his military career was short-lived, and he ended up working on the railroads, traveling widely through the Midwest and the South. Eventually, he opened a gas station in Corbin, Kentucky, which in the pre-interstate days was the main thoroughfare heading north. He added a family dining room and eventually a motel to his service station, and Sanders Service Station and Café became one of the few places a driver could stop and eat before continuing his journey. Western Kentucky food writer Duncan Hines reviewed the Sanders Café in 1935, noting its "sizzling steaks, fried chicken, country ham, and hot biscuits."

Business boomed, and Sanders soon owned several local motels and stores. In 1935, Sanders was commissioned a "Kentucky Colonel" by then governor Ruby Laffoon. The title of Kentucky Colonel is bestowed by the governor in recognition of specific accomplishments or service to the state. The Honorable Order of Kentucky Colonels was established in 1932. Prior to that, there were only one thousand owners of the title. Laffoon sought to boost this number tremendously by appointing a further five thousand, one of whom was Harland Sanders. In addition to adopting the title of

The Sanders Café in Corbin commemorates one of the state's most famous dishes.

Colonel, Sanders went one step further, adopting the now famous image of the southern colonel. He was often seen driving around Corbin in his large Cadillac attired in his white suit.

Disaster struck in 1955 when the main highway was rerouted away from Corbin. With no traffic at his doorstep, Harland Sanders found himself almost penniless. Ever the entrepreneur and remembering that his fried chicken had gained a certain popularity, he and his wife packed up their car and set off traveling around the country, approaching individual restaurants with the idea of franchising his brand of fried chicken. At each location, he would unpack from the trunk of his car his pressure cooker, his skillets and his spices, ready to roll up his sleeves in the kitchen. Fast-forward several decades, and Kentucky Fried Chicken was a national chain, now mass-producing fried chicken that was an adaptation of Sanders's method. Harland Sanders became little more than a figurehead for the company, and in his latter years, he was said to have bemoaned the product being sold under his image. But that image remained profitable. It represented southern values, charm and home-style cooking.

When Sanders opened his first café, fried chicken was far from restaurant food. It was home cooking, and it represented something to the rural South that few outsiders could understand: "the homiest and humblest of Sunday meals." Sharing a meal of fried chicken with someone was the quintessential act of southern hospitality; it was allowing them a glimpse into your family life. Harland Sanders had spent enough time in the South to understand this. Whether intentional or not, he took this humble dish and made it famous worldwide, a symbol of Kentucky. Sadly, in doing so, the product changed to meet corporate needs through quantity and profit rather than the requirements of those gathered around the family kitchen table seeking a simple meal.

So, what is the secret to not just good but great fried chicken? Correctly fried chicken may, as Camille Glenn said, be "simplicity itself," but the preparation of it is anything but. From every person you ask, you are likely to receive a different answer as to the type of fat you should use, the mix of spices for the coating and how long to soak the chicken before frying. Some have even moved beyond the cast-iron skillet to use a commercially bought fryer, although this breaks with the idea that true fried chicken is not deep fried. One thing that they all will tell you, though, is that proper fried chicken cannot be rushed. Perfection takes time. And that is why few, if any, fast-food outlets can measure up to the homemade.

Kentuckian Ronni Lundy described proper fried chicken as having "a crust that is at once crisp and tender. When your teeth sink through it, the meat they find inside should be firm but succulent, bursting with hot juice and rich chicken flavor." The coating should not be greasy and soggy, nor should it be fried to such crispiness that it shatters upon first bite. The chicken should be meaty, with clear form—no nugget-style ground remnants here. It should be savored in good company, not wolfed down on the way home from work.

Fried Chicken

As mentioned earlier, every cook has his or her own way of preparing fried chicken. John T. Edge insisted that the chicken pieces be soaked in ice water to remove any blood. Some cooks will soak the meat in buttermilk for several hours, while others insist on just the lightest dip before coating in flour. The type of fat used creates further debate: lard, bacon grease and peanut oil are probably the most commonly used, but vegetable, grapeseed and even coconut oil may be used. Butter will burn and is no good. Then there is the coating. This, to me and to the overwhelming majority of Kentuckians, is nonnegotiable. Ignore the misguided urge to use breadcrumbs unless you intend to make Maryland-style chicken. All you need for the perfect crunch is some flour and a few spices.

1 chicken, cut into segments
water or buttermilk (optional)
1 cup flour
salt, pepper or other spices
fat for cooking

Soak the chicken portions in water or buttermilk, if you choose, but be sure to then pat the meat dry. Place in a bag with the flour and spices. Shake enough to coat the chicken.

In a cast-iron skillet, heat enough fat to provide 1½ to 2 inches in depth when melted. Hot oil is key, so be sure that it is good and hot before you add the meat. There should be a violent sizzling when the meat is added to the oil. Whether to leave the pan uncovered while the meat cooks is again a personal preference, but once again I defer to Mr. Edge, cooking for 5 minutes on each side uncovered and then 5 minutes on each side covered. Place the chicken on a wire rack in a low-temperature oven while cooking the rest of the chicken. I find that this helps to keep the coating nice and crisp.

Chicken Gravy

Should you like gravy with your fried chicken (and who doesn't?), this is a perfect side. It also goes well with mashed potatoes.

2 tablespoons of leftover drippings from frying the chicken
2 tablespoons flour
1½ cups milk

Chicken and Dumplings

The dumplings in this winter favorite are very different from English-style dumplings, which are dropped into the broth by spoonful to form light, fluffy rounds. Kentucky-style dumplings are rolled and cut into thin strips before being placed in the stew to cook.

1 whole chicken
1 large onion, sliced
2 carrots, sliced
salt and pepper
1 teaspoon thyme

1 cup flour
2 teaspoons baking powder
¼ teaspoon salt
¼ cup milk
1 egg (optional)

Place the chicken, onion and carrots in a Dutch oven and cover with water. Bring the water to a boil and cook until the chicken is done, about 1 hour. Remove the chicken from the pan and, when cool, strip the meat from the bones. Return the meat to the broth. Add salt, pepper and thyme to suit your tastes. Bring the broth back to a boil. To make the dumplings, sift the dry ingredients together. Add milk (and egg, if using) to create a dough. Roll out on a floured surface to about ¼-inch thickness. Then cut into strips. Drop into the boiling stew and cook for 10 to 15 minutes.

Where there are chickens, there'll be eggs, and so it is at the Kentucky dinner table. So popular they merit their own specific serving tray, complete with indentations to hold each egg, the deviled egg (or, as some churchgoing folk prefer, the dressed egg) is a standard at picnics, meals, church events and so on. It may not have originated in Kentucky, or even in the United States, but it is certainly considered southern.

The idea of boiling eggs and eating with pepper dates back to Roman times, and by the thirteenth century, Spanish cooks were stuffing them with an assortment of herbs, spices, raisins and cheese. Flash-forward some three or four hundred years later, and mustard seemed to be a fairly standard part of the filling. The term "deviled" first appeared in the eighteenth century to describe food that had been highly seasoned. By the nineteenth century, one could find recipes for deviled kidneys, deviled ham and, of course, deviled eggs. Recipes for them in nineteenth-century cookbooks are few and far between. Even cookbooks from the early twentieth century have a tendency to list them under other names. Mrs. Dull offered a recipe for stuffed eggs, the stuffing comprising mustard, pickles and bacon. Marion Flexner shared a friend's recipe for Eggs Derby, in which the hard-boiled eggs are cut in half and the yolks mixed with cream, sweetbreads and mushrooms before being topped with cheese and reheated in the oven.

Deviled Eggs

Most modern recipes for deviled eggs follow the same basic recipe, with a few personal variations as taste dictates.

1 dozen eggs	2 tablespoons pickle relish
¼ cup mayonnaise	salt and pepper
2 teaspoons mustard	paprika or cayenne pepper

Hard-boil the eggs. When cooked, rinse them under cold water, remove the shells and cut in half. Carefully scoop the yolks into a bowl. Mash together the yolks with the mayonnaise, mustard and relish. Add salt and pepper to taste. Spoon the yolk mix back into the egg whites and sprinkle with paprika or cayenne pepper.

FISH AND FROGS

Both men and women fished the creeks for trout and other small fish on Stoney Fork, and in Straight Creek, which fed into the Cumberland River, for catfish.
—Sidney Saylor Farr, More than Moonshine

Without any coastline, Kentucky may be lacking in seafood, but its waterways more than make up for that with a plethora of fish and other riverside creatures. More than two hundred other varieties of fish can all be caught in both the mountain streams of the east and the larger rivers and lakes of the west. Carp and trout were both introduced in the 1800s.

Methods of fishing varied from the legal to the illegal. Some fishermen used trotlines, which they would regularly check and rebait. Others tried their hands at a practice known as noodling, remarkably similar to tickling trout. This involved putting one's hands in the water into the nooks where a catfish might be lurking. A skilled noodler could catch a lot of fish, but unlike trout, catfish can cause a fair scrape when they fight back. *Food and Everyday Family Life on Kentucky Farms* recalls one common type of illegal trap used by fishermen from the 1880s to the 1930s:

The trap consisted of a stone weir with two diagonal walls across the river. The weir was open, with a space of about eight feet between two abutments of carefully stacked rocks. There was a sluice in back of the opening with diagonal baffles to stop the fish. The trap was set up to allow smaller fish to pass through to catch larger fish, such as catfish, carp, gar, spoonbill, and punkin seeds.

The poor catfish has long been dismissed by some simply because of its reputation as a bottom feeder, but it is, without a doubt, the fish of the South. What could be more southern than a plate of fried catfish, hush puppies and coleslaw? Many Kentucky churches still have a Friday night fish fry, and catfish

A man fishing the waters of Kentucky. *Louis Edward Nollau Nitrate Photographic Print Collection, University of Kentucky.*

is often the fish of choice. Mary Randolph shared a recipe for catfish soup in *The Virginia Housewife* (provided here) while expressing her disappointment at those who have "imbibed a needless prejudice against those delicious fish."

Catfish Soup

Take two large or four small white catfish that have been caught in deep water, cut off the heads, and skin and clean the bodies; cut each in three parts, put them in a pot, with a pound of lean bacon, a large onion cut up, a handful of parsley chopped small, some pepper and salt, pour in a sufficient quantity of water, and stew them till the fish are quite tender but not broken; beat the yelks [sic] of four fresh eggs, add to them a large spoonful of butter, two of flour, and half a pint of rich milk; make all these warm and thicken the soup, take out the bacon, and put some of the fish in your tureen, pour in the soup, and serve it up.

Lettice Bryan's Fried Catfish

Cut and season them…; dredge them with flour and fry them a handsome brown in boiling lard. Serve them up warm, stir into a gravy a handful of chopped parsley, a spoonful of flour, a tea-spoonful of cayenne pepper and a glass of sweet cream; shake it up, and pour it at once over the steaks.

You would be remiss to have fried catfish without a side of hush puppies, which reputedly originated with fishermen farther south, who would fry bits of leftover cornmeal to silence their dogs, although others claim that they date farther back, to the days of Daniel Boone.

Hush Puppies

2 cups cornmeal
2 teaspoons baking powder
1 teaspoon salt
1 egg
⅔ cup milk
1 onion, chopped

Combine all the ingredients and roll pieces of dough into pieces resembling golf balls in size. Fry in hot fat.

The average visitor to Kentucky might be rather surprised to find frog legs available alongside the fried catfish on the buffet at most state parks, but our amphibian friends also have their spot in Kentucky dining history. In 1940, fried frog legs featured on the Christmas Day menu of Louisville's Brown Hotel. More than seventy years later, they can still be found at state park restaurants. Thought to be of French origin, there is now a surprising amount of evidence that the liking for frog legs may have actually originated in the area known today as England, perhaps as early as 7000 BC. Even way back then, they were probably caught in much the same way as they are today: frog gigging. Gigging is a popular pastime in Kentucky, and many a young boy has joined his friends or his dad for a night's frog hunting. Although other fish can be caught with the gig, which is a multi-pronged spear, here in Kentucky, the bullfrog is the main prize. Frogs can be hunted during the day, but night is preferred. Shine a flashlight into their eyes to

Lexington's Parkette has been offering poor boys, fried chicken and fish boxes since 1951. *The Parkette.*

Stebbins Grill in Louisville boasted about its variety of seafood shipped daily from New England. *Postcard Collection at the University of Kentucky.*

stun them and then move in for the kill. The frog's legs are fried and eaten, an excellent addition to the breakfast biscuits and eggs. Mary Harris Frazer offered the following method for preparing them:

Select fresh frogs, trim off the feet. Put in a bowl 2 teaspoons of olive oil, 2 teaspoons vinegar, pepper and salt. Place the legs in this dressing for 15 minutes. Make a batter with 2 eggs, beaten light, 1½ teacups of flour, 1 cup new milk and a little salt. Beat well, then add 1 teaspoon baking powder. Dip the legs in this batter; fry in very hot lard about 6 minutes. Serve with Tartare sauce and parsley.

The Southern Cook Book of Fine Old Recipes offers a simple dish of breaded fried frog legs, calling it "A Dish for the Epicure." I wonder if they knew how much gourmet delight the humble Kentuckian was already enjoying. Today in Kentucky, a license is required for frog gigging. The season runs for five months during the summer, and each license holder is permitted to catch up to fifteen bullfrogs per day.

Oysters

Thomas D. Clark once wrote, "There can be little doubt but that Kentuckians know how to dine. Their historical definition of a good dinner is, 'a turkey at one end of the table, a ham at the other, six vegetables down one side, and seven down the other with pickles and jelly sprinkled in between, and with a side dish of oysters.'"

Even the earliest Kentucky cookbooks contain numerous recipes for preparing oysters; they appear fried, in soups, in stuffing for meat dishes and in sauces, ketchup and even omelets. But where on earth would residents of this landlocked state obtain oysters back in the early 1800s? The answer seems to have been: by whatever means you could. In the coastal states of the colonies, oysters would have been as readily available as other fish and seafood. Once settlers moved to Kentucky, they relied on stagecoaches to bring deliveries of oysters. Since these deliveries would have been few and far between, this no doubt explains how oysters became a menu item at fancy feasts and Christmas. Once the railroads developed, they could be shipped more easily, in huge barrels of ice, but they still would have been rather expensive, ensuring their continued place on the festive dinner table.

Oyster Casserole

An oyster casserole frequently makes an appearance at the Thanksgiving or Christmas table.

½ cup butter
1 onion, finely chopped
¼ cup parsley
salt and pepper
2 tablespoons lemon juice

1 teaspoon Worcestershire sauce
3 cups saltine crackers
1 quart oysters
1 cup cream

Melt the butter and sauté the onion until soft. Add the parsley, salt, pepper, lemon juice, Worcestershire sauce and crushed crackers. Layer the oysters and the breadcrumb mix in a dish until you have about ½ cup of the breadcrumb mix remaining. Pour the cream over the layers and top with the remaining breadcrumbs. Bake at 350° F for about 40 minutes.

For many generations, tobacco was the prime cash crop for Kentucky farmers, but with quotas having been cut significantly over the last decade or so, many have found themselves wondering what to plant instead. Few options seemed a suitable replacement. After all, tobacco was easy to grow, easy to sell and had a high yield per acre, which translated into a profitable crop. Few vegetable crops could meet that level of profit, and livestock require more land. What does this have to do with fish, you might ask. In the last few years of the twentieth century, the state began trying to encourage farmers to adopt of new form of agriculture, or rather aquaculture. The movement has been slow to gain traction, but those who have made the change are now raising shrimp, catfish, tilapia and a few other varieties. Whereas an acre of farmland might yield 2,500 pounds of tobacco at perhaps $2 per pound, an acre of water can yield 1,000 pounds of shrimp at as much as $9 per pound. Competing with cheaper Asian imports is hard, but with growing interest in supporting local farmers, perhaps shrimp and grits will one day be a Kentucky tradition after all.

PART IV
BEVERAGES

BOURBON AND MOONSHINE

You can't discuss Kentucky's food heritage without mentioning bourbon. Generations of Scottish and Irish immigrants settled in the Appalachian Mountains and the Bluegrass. In the Old Country, they had developed methods of distilling surplus grain into liquor. Pretty soon, they missed their favorite tipple from back home: whiskey. In fact, at the time of Kentucky's birth as a state, the average American drank two and a half gallons of spirits per year (plus wine and beer). There was clearly a demand for whiskey, but there was a problem. There just didn't seem to be any rye around. Being an ingenious bunch, they soon figured out how to put corn to good use; remember that the growing of corn was one of the requirements in the Virginia land laws. The Kentucky soil, limestone water, corn supply and availability of wood all came together, and bourbon was born.

The naming of bourbon is often credited to the Reverend Elijah Craig, a Baptist minister who began distilling the corn liquor in what is now Georgetown in 1786 or thereabouts. Others dispute this on the grounds that Georgetown was not in Bourbon County, and so Craig was unlikely to have named his product for a nearby county rather than his own. These historians

Whiskey must be aged in oak barrels to be considered
bourbon. *Buffalo Trace.*

Buffalo Trace Distillery, established in 1786, was
designated a National Historic Landmark in 2013.
Buffalo Trace.

claim that the name came from the fact that corn whiskey was shipped from Bourbon County and thereby picked up the name "Old Bourbon." It became popular elsewhere, and people began to ask for bourbon, and soon the name was used for any Kentucky corn whiskey. To be fair, both sides are correct. Bourbon County was once a much greater expanse of land than it is now and encompassed what would, in 1792, become Scott County (with Georgetown as its county seat). It also stretched as far as the Ohio River for those who claim that shipping by river from Bourbon County would not have been likely. In the county as it is today, perhaps, but not so in Kentucky's infancy.

Whatever story you believe about the origin of the name, a few things are ensured by law. Bourbon can only be made in the United States, it must be at least 51 percent corn and it must be aged for at least two years in new, charred oak barrels. Not until 1870 or thereabouts did bourbon begin to be bottled. Prior to that, it stayed in the barrel.

By 1810, there were two thousand distilleries in the state of Kentucky. Whiskey was an important commodity in those days. Along with ginseng, it was one of the few local commodities that could be traded down the Ohio River or across the Cumberland Gap into Virginia and still have a profit after transportation costs were accounted for. It also served a key role in the bartering economy. In the early days, whiskey was as good as cash in many business transactions. When Abraham Lincoln's father, Thomas, sold his Kentucky farm to move to Indiana, the payment he received for the land was twenty dollars and ten barrels of whiskey. Kentucky bourbon was also highly prized in New Orleans; by 1819, as many as 200,000 gallons passed through the port each month.

The business had its ups and downs through the nineteenth century, but the biggest hit came in 1919 with the enactment of the Volstead Act, the start of Prohibition. A small number of distilleries, such as Buffalo Trace and Four Roses, were allowed to continue operating, producing bourbon for medicinal purposes, but most shut their doors. Some distilleries restarted once Prohibition had ended. The family behind Jim Beam spent the Prohibition era in Florida growing citrus, but they returned as soon as they could to start distilling again. They continued to be as successful as ever, and there were even some new distilleries—Heaven Hill, for example. In a strange twist of fate, many of the distilleries were in counties that remained dry after Prohibition, meaning that it was made in the county, but none of the residents could buy it. Few bourbon distilleries could compete as the twentieth century progressed. By the 1970s, whiskey was no longer the best-selling liquor in the United States. Distilleries

A 1938 ad for Ancient Age bourbon. *Buffalo Trace.*

were struggling. Fortunately, they have since rebounded. In 2000, Labrot and Graham's Old Oscar Pepper Distillery in Versailles, homes of Woodford Reserve, was appointed a National Historic Landmark. The distillery is the only one locally to still use a copper pot for distillation.

Kentucky continues to celebrate its bourbon heritage and something of a bourbon revival. The annual Bourbon Festival, held in Bardstown every September, is a week filled with tastings and events to celebrate Kentucky's finest. In addition, the Bourbon Trail offer tours that teach about the history of bourbon and show visitors the ins and outs of the distilling process.

Although bourbon can legally be distilled anywhere in the United States, 95 percent is from Kentucky. So, whether you drink it neat or in a mint julep, when you're enjoying bourbon, chances are you're tasting Kentucky history. Speaking of which, were you aware of the controversy behind something as simple as the mint julep?

The julep began as a medicinal drink, imbibed to ward off fevers. The name is believed to have derived from the Persian *gulab* and the Arabic *julab*, both meaning rosewater. Early versions were based on English juleps, containing wine or brandy and fruit. Elizabeth Ross speculated that poor southerners, who could not afford such fine liquor, switched to the readily available bourbon. If this is true, one cannot help but admire the irony that the mint julep is now unquestionably a bourbon-based drink.

I have heard of a legend that a boatman "discovered" the mint julep when he was searching near the Mississippi for some spring water to mix with his bourbon, found some fresh mint growing and decided to toss some in. As charming as the story may be, historians are almost all in agreement that the drink as we know it originated among genteel Virginia society in the early eighteenth century.

The mint julep "requires the best of everything if you would have it in perfection." Sadly, the advice of Martha McCulloch-Williams often goes ignored now, with premade mixers taking the place of fresh mint and sugar. McCulloch-Williams called for the sugar and water to be set on ice for at least six hours so that the sugar would be properly dissolved. Of course, she also called for lemon zest to be rubbed around the rim of the glass and for the addition of a ripe strawberry or cherry, things that would cause the modern julep connoisseur to cringe. Nevertheless, she is correct in her demand for the best; the freshest mint and the finest bourbon should be used.

But how to handle the mint? Herein lies the controversial nature of the mint julep. Should it be carefully handled, or should the leaves be bruised so that the flavors can escape? Lexington lawyer Soule Smith wrote an ode to the beloved drink, advising that "[l]ike a woman's heart, mint gives its sweetest aroma when bruised." On the other hand, Irvin Cobb wrote that "[a]ny guy who'd put rye in a mint julep and crush the leaves would put scorpions in a baby's bed." Clearly a contentious topic.

Today, the mint julep seems to have been relegated to a once-a-year Kentucky Derby celebratory drink, and even then, it is rarely made with the care it deserves. Although if you have a spare $1,000 and happen to be at Churchill Downs on Derby Day, you might wish to partake of Woodford Reserve's special mint julep for charity. Served in a limited-edition silver julep cup and gold-plated straw (both of which you keep), one year's version contained mint from Morocco, ice from the Arctic Circle and sugar from the South Pacific. Should you choose to enjoy a proper (and more affordable) julep at home, here is statesman Henry Clay's rather poetic recipe and a more straightforward one. Traditionally, the mint julep was served in a silver cup; most of us make do with a glass.

Henry Clay's Mint Julep

The mint leaves, fresh and tender, should be pressed against a coin-silver goblet with the back of a silver spoon. Only bruise the leaves gently and then remove them from the goblet. Half fill with cracked ice. Mellow bourbon, aged in oaken barrels, is poured from the jigger and allowed to slice slowly through the cracked ice.

In another receptacle, granulated sugar is slowly mixed into chilled limestone water to make a silvery mixture as smooth as some rare Egyptian oil, then poured on top of the ice. While beads of moisture gather on the burnished exterior of the silver goblet, garnish the brim of the goblet with choicest springs of mint.

Mint Julep

4 sprigs fresh mint
1 teaspoon powdered sugar
2 teaspoons water
2½ ounces bourbon
crushed ice

Put the mint, sugar and water in a glass and muddle. Top with bourbon and lots of crushed ice. Garnish with an extra mint sprig.

To imbibe this drink, may I suggest also following the advice of Soule Smith:

Then when it is made, sip it slowly…It is fragrant, cold and sweet—it is seductive. No maiden's kiss is tenderer or more refreshing, no maiden's touch could be more passionate… Sip it and say there is no solace for the soul, no tonic for the body like old Bourbon whiskey.

The cocktail may be thought of as a relatively modern invention, but it has been around in one form or another since the mid-eighteenth century. The earliest cocktails were a simple mix of sugar, water, bitters and liquor. Within one hundred years or so, bartenders were becoming more creative, adding flavored syrups and cordials. Although this ingenuity led to some wonderful drinks, gentlemen began to long for the simplicity of days gone by, and by 1870, they were asking for an old-fashioned drink, meaning the original sugar syrup and bitters. At this point in time, the use of "old-fashioned" did not refer to a specific drink, just the style of making the drink.

The Pendennis Club in Louisville is an exclusive gentlemen's club, first established in 1881. Colonel James E. Pepper, a noted bourbon distiller, was a member. Although the exact date remains rather vague—somewhere between 1889 and 1895—Pepper asked the club's bartender, Martin Cuneo, to make him an old-fashioned drink, and the Old Fashioned cocktail, as we know it today, was born. Pepper would later introduce the drink to New York society, and in 1895, it began appearing in cocktail recipe books.

Old Fashioned (as Created at the Pendennis Club)

½ ounce sugar syrup
Angostura bitters
orange slice
lemon twist
cherry
2½ ounces bourbon

Place the syrup, bitters and fruit in a glass. Muddle. Add the bourbon.

Moonshine

I'll eat when I'm hungry and drink when I'm dry;
If moonshine don't kill me, I'll live 'til I die...

—*moonshiner (traditional)*

The term "moonshine" may be thought of as all-American, but it originated at both ends of the British Isles—both the southern coast and Scotland and Ireland—in the seventeenth century. Taxes imposed on liquor imports meant that smugglers, or moonshiners, stayed busy sneaking barrels across marshes, into caves and past the eye of the revenuer. Now, of course, moonshine refers to the drink itself, and those who make or smuggle it are known as bootleggers.

In the days when Reverend Elijah Craig and Evan Williams were making their first batches of whiskey, anyone could distill liquor, and many no doubt did. After all, the land laws required that settlers grew corn, and they needed a use for the leftovers. Early attempts by Alexander Hamilton to tax whiskey met with staunch opposition; by 1800, some 177 Kentucky moonshiners had been prosecuted. The tax was later repealed, but in 1862, the government created a new tax, a wartime excise tax. It was then that a sharp division was created between those distillers who paid the tax and would become legitimate businesses and those who refused and whose unaged whiskey became moonshine. Over the years, moonshine kept its popularity, despite the rise of legally distilled and aged bourbon. For one thing, it was cheaper than its increasingly taxed cousin, and it took a fraction of the time to be ready. No aging in oak barrels for this liquor; simply distill corn and sugar, pour into a jar and drink.

Then Prohibition came, and moonshining became really big business. In Kentucky, the legal and illegal distillation of liquor stood side by side, since several distilleries were permitted to continue production, despite the Constitutional amendment, for medicinal purposes, bourbon being a prescribed elixir for nerves. One can only imagine how many more "nervous" people there must have been during the 1920s. Moonshiners were under pressure to meet greater demand during Prohibition. Suddenly, mountain farmers, who typically made enough for themselves and perhaps a little to sell when times were hard, now found themselves in a situation where everybody wanted some. Organized crime and those seeking to make their fortunes entered the field, and this is where moonshine became dangerous. Whereas those who'd been distilling it for generations knew what they were doing, the newcomers produced mostly low-quality alcohol. Blindness, paralysis and other crippling results were down to mob racketeering rather than the old man in the holler. Nevertheless, moonshine developed something of a reputation that stayed with it for the next few decades.

Even after the repeal of Prohibition, moonshine continued to sell well. High taxation meant that the illicitly produced alternative could undercut legal options. For example, David Maurer found that a gallon of good-quality moonshine could sell for ten dollars in Bardstown during the 1950s, even more nearer the Tennessee border in Glasgow. Furthermore, so many counties within Kentucky remained dry, even after repeal, that liquor could still not be bought legally.

But in the last few years, something odd has happened: moonshine has become legit. A recent rise in microdistilleries (legal and licensed) has seen a growing interest in producing not just small-batch bourbons, vodkas and other spirits but also white whiskey (as it is called since it has not aged). Now people across the country can claim the thrill of drinking something with an illicit past when they are, in truth, drinking something very legal. Although much of it is produced in Tennessee, Kentucky has its own brands, including Devil John, made in Lexington, and LBL in Hardin County.

Moonshine gave more to the people of the United States than just illegal liquor and a lasting image of the bootlegger; it also led to the nation's most popular spectator sport. And although Kentucky cannot take sole credit, I like to think that those moonshiners speeding through the curvy mountain roads of eastern Kentucky played their part. Both during and after Prohibition, a bootlegger's wily knowledge of the local lanes could only go so far in protecting him from the revenuers. When it came to a chase, he needed to rely on some mechanical know-how to make his getaway car just that little bit faster. Pretty soon, this led to informal races between bootleggers throughout the South, all keen to earn bragging rights as to who was the fastest. In 1947, a meeting was held down in Florida, and the National Association for Stock Car Auto Racing was born. Many of the early professional NASCAR drivers were former bootleggers. Today's drivers, some descended from those first racers, lead much more glamorous lives of multimillion-dollar sponsorship deals and supermodel girlfriends. But the next time you watch a race, be sure to sip a little moonshine and remember that the roots of NASCAR run through the hollers.

SWEET TEA AND SODEY-POP

Sweet tea—your mother's sweet tea—means you are home.
—*Fred Thompson*

Shortly after graduating college, my husband traveled to Japan, where he spent three years teaching English. He took with him a plentiful supply of books, a large box of tea bags and his mother's recipe for sweet tea. Years later, when we married, his mother gave me a plastic pitcher, just for making tea. Handing it to me with the gravity of a Nobel Prize, she carefully explained the process of making this highly prized elixir. Later, my husband would show me how to make it, again with the seriousness that I have come to learn is expected when discussing sweet tea.

More recently, my sister-in-law expressed outrage when, during a trip to Arizona, she was unable to find sweet tea at any restaurant. Horrified by the blank looks, she indignantly declared that she was from Kentucky, where they know how to make tea.

Sweet tea is serious business. And I have a confession, one that may demand that my Kentucky residency be revoked: it's too sweet for me.

Non-southern friends have been known to sample a refreshing glass of my mother-in-law's recipe for sweet tea and claim to have suffered instant diabetic shock, such is the quantity of sugar contained therein. It may seem an all-too-obvious question: why not omit the sugar and add it to your glass as you see fit? Such a question is met with a shake of the head and a look of pity. "She ain't from 'round here. She don't understand."

The sugar does not dissolve properly when added to cold liquid. It tastes different. Therefore, the only proper way to make sweet tea is to add the sugar to the warm brewing tea. And make sure it's proper sugar—none of those artificial substances that come in paper packets. As for how much sugar, it is best summed up by Hilary Kraus: "Although Southerners' tea to sugar preference ranges in ratio, one rule is universal: The tea must contain enough sugar…to keep a small village amped up for weeks."

There you have the steadfast rule of sweet tea. While you will come across one hundred or more different ways to make it—whether to add cold water, what type of jug it must be made in and so on—it must contain plenty of the sweet stuff.

The invention of iced tea is widely credited to the 1904 World's Fair in St. Louis. As temperatures soared, thirsty fair patrons desired something more cooling than the available beverages. An enterprising man had the idea of serving iced tea, and the drink was a rousing success. While the World's Fair may have introduced many to the concept of iced tea, it was certainly already commonplace in the South and Kentucky in one form or another.

Probably the earliest known version of a cold tea was tea punch, a rich concoction of tea, sugar, cream and liquor, as shared in Lettice Bryan's *The Kentucky Housewife*, written in 1839.

Lettice Bryan's Tea Punch

1½ pints strong tea
1¼ pounds loaf sugar (an estimated 2½ cups)
½ pint of rich cream
1 bottle claret or champagne

Strain the tea and pour over the sugar while still boiling hot. Add the cream and then gradually add the claret or champagne, stirring carefully. The punch may then be reheated to boiling or may be served cold.

Later in the nineteenth century, Mrs. S.T. shared a recipe in *Housekeeping in Old Virginia* that comprised green tea and a quart of boiling water. It was made in the morning and left to stand until tea time, at which point the cooled beverage was poured over ice and sugar. A squeeze of lemon was also suggested. This recipe was followed a few years later by one using black tea. As black tea grew in popularity, eventually eclipsing its green cousin, so iced tea changed to incorporate what was available. By the time the 1904 World's Fair took place, many housewives, at least in the South, already knew the joys of a sweet glass of iced tea.

Mother-in-Law's Iced Tea

In all fairness to my mother-in-law, I later discovered that my husband had, in fact, erred in his tea making, adding as many as five half-cup scoops of sugar! Here is the recipe as it should be.

11 cups water
½ cup sugar (add more or less to suit taste)
8 tea bags

Bring 3 cups water and sugar to a rolling boil. Remove from heat and add the tea bags. Cover and let steep for 30 minutes. Pour into a pitcher and top up with 8 cups of cold water. Chill. Can be served with or without lemon.

A Late One?

Pop, soda, cola. The name you give your carbonated drink of choice will often depend on the part of the country from which you hail. Maps from dialect studies proclaim that in eastern Kentucky it is "pop," while everywhere else it is "coke." In truth, judging from those I've spoken to across the state, the answers are much more varied, and, as if to prove the extreme regionality of names, my husband calls it "sodey-pop," a term I have yet to hear another Kentuckian use.

Regardless of what moniker you choose, soft drinks are mighty popular, and Kentucky references range from the good (Coca-Cola cake) to the bad (the famed "Mountain Dew Mouth" that is allegedly damaging Appalachians' teeth). For more than a decade, Pikeville, Hazard and Corbin ranked highest in the nation for per capita consumption of Pepsi, in part due to poor local water quality.

It seems that every state has its own regional soft drink, and Kentucky is no exception. Carbonated soft drinks predate the Civil War. Dr. Joseph Priestley created the first drinkable man-made fizzy water in the late eighteenth century. Shortly thereafter, Jacob Schweppe began selling his Schweppes carbonated waters in three different varieties depending on the ailment; at this time, soda waters were considered beneficial to one's health. Over the next few decades, the methods of adding carbonation spread to America, and various contraptions were devised for creating soda waters. Flavors such as ginger or lemon, again seen as medicinal, were occasionally added. However, the drinks truly came into their own in the 1880s. In 1886, Georgia pharmacist John Pemberton invented Coca-Cola, the first cola drink. Many of the original soda pops, which as John Egerton has pointed out got their name from the sound of the cork popping out of the bottle, began as pharmaceutical tonics. Once pharmacists realized how popular they were as a refreshing drink, they entered a whole new market.

In 1902, G.L. Wainscott decided to enter the drink business with flavored soda waters, bottled at his small business in Winchester. Cola drinks were gaining popularity, and everyone wanted a piece of the profit pie, including Wainscott. So, in 1906, he introduced Roxa-Kola. However, a few companies were quickly dominating the cola market and were using their size to push smaller manufacturers out of the market. If they couldn't beat them with sales, they would take court action, causing many businesses to fold rather than face a lengthy legal battle. Although Wainscott prevailed in court, he was smart enough to see the writing on the wall. He knew that his

Kentucky's own soda: Ale-8-One. *Ale-8-One.*

competitors would continue their attempts to drive him out of business. He needed something new. Something unique.

During his travels in Europe, Wainscott had come across a variety of different ginger beers. He created a citrus and ginger formula, but it needed a name. He held a contest at the local county fair, and in 1926, Ale-8-One was named, a pun on "A Late One" as the latest thing in soft drinks. Business thrived. Production of Roxa-Kola continued until 1968 and other flavored sodas until 1974, but it has been Ale-8-One that made Wainscott's fortune. The formula remains a closely guarded secret, although visitors to the Winchester plant are allowed a sniff of the mystical concentrated brew. In 2003, a diet version was introduced, followed by a caffeine-free version in 2011. Ale-8-One is widely available in Ohio, Indiana and Kentucky, as well as some outlets farther afield.

PART V

SOMETHING SWEET

SORGHUM: THE SWEET BEHIND IT ALL

A visit to any historic house in Kentucky might reveal a curious piece of furniture: the sugar chest. Usually found in either the dining room or the living room (never the kitchen), this stored one of the household's most precious commodities. Sugar was expensive in colonial America, and thus its use was restricted to the wealthiest of families. To ensure that not one ounce was wasted and that it remained safe from moisture, it was kept under lock and key, the mistress of the house keeping a careful eye on the stock, chipping some off for the cook to use as needed. It should be noted that the sugar was purchased in ten-pound blocks, and deliveries were few and far between, so the chest was able to hold a decent amount.

Given the high price of sugar and the fact that it cannot grow in areas that suffer a frost, such as Kentucky, the average family relied on molasses. Although there are sticklers who insist that true molasses refers only to that produced by crystallizing sugar cane, in Kentucky sorghum syrup is known as sorghum molasses. In his 1944 book *Pills, Petticoats, and Plows*, Thomas D. Clark called sorghum molasses the "lowest"

The man who cooked sorghum went from one farmhouse to another, taking a share of the syrup for his work. *Marion Post Wolcott, 1940, Library of Congress.*

Pouring off and straining sorghum near Campton, Kentucky. *Marion Post Wolcott, Library of Congress.*

grade molasses; many Kentuckians would beg to differ. The crop has been grown since colonial times; some say that Benjamin Franklin first introduced it to this country. Despite the aforementioned failure by the Shakers to grow Chinese sorghum successfully (one can only speculate as to whether the soil contained too much clay), on the whole, sorghum cane was and continues to be greatly suited to the Kentucky climate. Able to tolerate both drought and high temperatures, it grows well in fertilized Kentucky loam.

According to Rona Roberts, a Kentucky food writer and sorghum aficionado, sorghum cane probably originated in Africa, although stories vary. At one point in time, sorghum was a major crop in the commonwealth; in 1899, the first year sorghum crop statistics were recorded, almost twenty-two thousand acres were grown, resulting in more than 1 million gallons of syrup. Production decreased in the twentieth century, and by 1972, fewer than five hundred acres were devoted to the crop.

Sorghum harvesting time was often an event that involved the entire community. Dr. Daniel Drake described the wheat harvests of his childhood as "a social labour, a frolic, a scene of excitement." We can surmise that the sorghum harvest had a similar sense of excitement. Sorghum cooks would travel from one farm to the next, trading their expertise in cooking the syrup for a jar of the delicious final product. Children would take the day off school, and neighbors would come by, all hoping for the first drop of sweetness. The sorghum cook would begin shortly after daybreak. A large, deep vat was set over a fire. Just keeping the fire going was a job in itself. In the field, men cut the sorghum, stripping the leaves away and piling the canes high in wagons to be taken to the gristmill. The cut sorghum cane was passed through the mill to extract the juice. After straining, the juice was added to the vat for cooking.

Making the molasses was a slow process, and the experienced sorghum cookers kept a watchful eye on the vat of juice as it boiled down to syrup. They used large wooden paddles to stir it, watching it as it changed in color from vivid green to dark amber, the total mass shrinking by as much as 90 percent. As the sun sank lower in the sky, the crowd gathered around the vat, knowing that the time had nearly come. Eventually, the cook would announce that it was just right. Then would start the runoff process; jars and jugs were filled to the brim with the newly cooked sorghum molasses. Hot biscuits and corn bread would be brought from the kitchen as an accompaniment for that first tasting. Often, there might be a celebration at the end of the work, with friends gathering to enjoy a successful sorghum harvest.

Although production declined dramatically in the twentieth century, there has been renewed interest in sorghum molasses as a locally produced product. Kentucky leads the nation in sorghum production, making more than $12 million worth of syrup in 2008. The community of West Liberty holds an annual sorghum festival every year.

Pulled Sorghum Candy

One of the simplest old-fashioned candy recipes, this requires nothing more than sorghum molasses, a dab of soda and some elbow grease.

4 cups sorghum molasses
¼ teaspoon soda

Cook the sorghum until it can be spun into threads (about 232° F if using a candy thermometer). Remove from the heat, add the soda and beat the sorghum until it thickens. Pour into a lightly greased pan and leave to cool. When cool, pull into long taffy strings. Allow to harden before cutting into pieces.

Mrs. Fisher's Ginger Cookies

Sorghum makes an excellent substitute for traditional sugar molasses in the following recipe from Mrs. Abby Fisher:

> *One teacup of molasses, one-half teacup of sugar, one tablespoonful of butter, one tablespoonful of lard, one quart of flour, two tablespoonfuls of ginger, one teaspoonful of cinnamon, one teaspoonful of allspice, two tablespoonfuls of yeast powder. Cream butter and sugar together and add molasses. Sift yeast powder and flour together and add to butter, sugar and molasses, then add lard and spices, etc., and work it up well. Roll out on a board, and cut them out and bake like you would a biscuit.*

Spice Cake

This version tweaks famed Louisville chef Jennie Benedict's spice cake recipe by substituting sorghum for molasses.

1 cup sugar	1 tablespoon cinnamon
½ cup sorghum	1 tablespoon ginger
½ cup butter	4 egg yolks, well beaten
½ cup sour milk	½ teaspoon cloves
2½ cups flour	½ teaspoon allspice
1 teaspoon baking soda	

Combine the ingredients and pour into a greased 9x12-inch pan. Bake at 325° F for half an hour.

BUTTER MY BISCUITS

A southern or mountain woman in my day was not worth much in the eyes of her family if she could not make good biscuits.
—Sidney Saylor Farr, *More than Moonshine*

In these days of convenience, when anyone can pick up a pop-open can of biscuits in the grocery store aisle, it can be all too easy to forget the taste of a homemade biscuit. When visiting relatives in eastern Kentucky, every meal is still accompanied by hot corn bread, fresh biscuits or both. Small wonder that it used to be said that a good biscuit could save a marriage.

In the days before flour and leavening, corn bread was king, but it later faced competition from the biscuit—and with good reason. Whether spread with butter, drizzled with sorghum molasses, filled with country ham or sausage or smothered with any one of the possible gravies, a biscuit is a satisfying breakfast or a suitable dinner accompaniment. But there was a time when the biscuit had strong class and economic implications in Appalachia, as Elizabeth Engelhardt has documented.

At the dawn of the twentieth century, a huge public health movement was underfoot in the United States. That movement soon made its way to poor, rural Kentucky, led by the efforts of Katherine Pettit and May Stone.

Born into a wealthy Fayette County family, Pettit became a teacher after studying for a few years at Lexington's prestigious Sayre School. May Stone also came from a privileged background, enjoying a private school education in Kentucky and then at Wellesley. Both women spent several summers teaching in the Hazard area and came to believe that they could open a school there, based on the type of settlement houses to be found in Chicago and other major cities. In 1902, they opened the Hindman Settlement School in Knott County, the first of its kind in the nation. Eleven years later, Pettit helped to found the Pine Mountain Settlement School in Harlan County. Within a few decades, public schools were established, and both Hindman and Pine Mountain changed their focus. Today, Hindman operates as an adult education center, and Pine Mountain specializes in environmental education. Pettit's legacy as an educator lives on in the region, and many have benefited from the programs offered by both schools over the course of a century. Fortunately for all of us, the women's views on corn bread are one legacy that did not endure.

The beaten biscuit—or, as Thomas D. Clark referred to it, the "blond sister" of the hardier corn bread—dates back to the nineteenth century and perhaps earlier. Known as "hardtack" or "sea biscuits" in the Northeast, they can be stored for several months. In the South, these thin biscuits are often filled with sliced country ham. Since they did not contain baking powder, soda or any other leavening agents, the cook needed to beat the dough vigorously for some time so that it would blister and achieve the proper consistency.

Corn bread was the bread of choice in turn-of-the-century eastern Kentucky. It was easily thrown together at a moment's notice by even the most inexperienced cook, whereas biscuits required a certain touch and a degree of time. In her journal, Pettit noted having to get up extra early to make beaten biscuits for a luncheon. One wonders where the average Appalachian housewife, already grossly overworked, was to find the time. To social reformers who had an erroneous tendency to conflate time in the kitchen and domesticity with health and morality, corn bread represented poverty, illiteracy and disease. The biscuit, on the other hand, was a positive image of consumption and goodness. Therefore, well-meaning "experts" sought to convert misguided Appalachians to civilization via the humble biscuit.

Wheat flour, the sort required for biscuits, was seen as an indicator of a better social class. However, what the reformers overlooked was that flour was very difficult for poor eastern Kentuckians to obtain. Corn could be easily grown, whereas wheat did not do well in the area. Buying it at the local store, if the store even stocked any, required money, and that was all too scarce. Even if flour could be obtained, there was then the matter of equipment, including a slab, preferably marble to cope with the repeated beatings, and a temperature-controlled oven. The alternative to beating by hand was a machine that resembled a laundry wringer—even more expensive. This was at a time when few mountain folks had more than a fireplace for cooking. Ultimately, in the eyes of the reformers, what separated the healthy from the unhealthy, the wealthy from the poor, were biscuits and corn bread.

Oddly enough, although Pettit and Stone worked hard educating women in the community about the virtues of the handmade beaten biscuit over corn bread, at Hindman Settlement students were served both at meals. Furthermore, the biscuits were machine-made.

Martha McCulloch-Williams's Beaten Biscuits

Sift a quart of flour into a bowl or tray, add half a teaspoon of salt, then cut small into it a teacup of very cold lard. Wet with cold water—ice water is best—into a very stiff dough. Lay on a floured block, or marble slab, and give one hundred strokes with a mallet or rolling pin. Fold afresh as the dough beats thin, dredging in flour if it begins to stick. The end of beating is to distribute air well through the mass, which, expanding by the heat of baking, makes the biscuit light. The dough should be firm, but smooth and very elastic. Roll to half-inch thickness, cut out with a small round cutter, prick lightly all over the top, and bake in steady heat to a delicate brown. Too hot an oven will scorch and blister, too cold an one [sic] make the biscuit hard and clammy.

Mrs. Dull instructed her readers to beat the dough for 20 minutes, Marion Cabell Tyree a steady half hour. Pettit and Stone recommended three hundred strokes when making biscuits for family. For guests, they preferred a more cumbersome five hundred strokes.

Today, most people are more familiar with the larger, fluffier, buttermilk biscuits. Although they do not require the aerobic exercise-style beating of their predecessors, they still require a certain amount of skill. Dale Curry offered the following advice about biscuit making: "All great biscuit makers will tell you that the handling of the dough has everything to do with it. Mix it but don't overwork it. Be gentle. Handle it like a newborn baby."

Mrs. Dull's Buttermilk Biscuits

2 cups flour	2 teaspoons baking powder
1 teaspoon salt	4 tablespoons shortening
½ teaspoon baking soda	1 cup buttermilk

Sift together the flour, salt, soda and baking powder. Cut in the shortening. Then add the buttermilk and stir to make a dough. Place on a floured board and knead until smooth. (This is where the gentle touch comes in.) Roll out to a half-inch thickness and cut into rounds. Bake in a 450° F oven for 10 minutes.

Chocolate Gravy

1½ cups sugar
2 tablespoons flour
2 tablespoons cocoa powder
2 cups water

Mix the ingredients together in a pan and cook until thickened. Serve with biscuits.

Sawmill Gravy

Sawmill gravy may once have been considered poor eating, but today you will find it on many menus as an accompaniment for country-fried steak or simply slopped over a freshly cooked biscuit. This is made after cooking breakfast sausage, using the dregs of the sausage and the leftover grease.

2–3 tablespoon grease (add more to the skillet if the leftovers
    from cooking sausage are not enough)
any leftover pieces of sausage in the pan
3 tablespoons flour
1 cup milk

Simply stir all together in the skillet and allow to thicken. If the sausage was good, additional seasoning probably won't be required.

BAKED GOODS

The most basic of cakes, the pound cake was introduced by the English in the 1700s. A recipe so simple that anyone could learn it, it contained one pound each of butter, flour, sugar and eggs and no doubt made a behemoth of a cake. But as long as the ratios remained the same—an equal weight of each ingredient—a smaller cake could be made. As well as being easy to remember, the simplicity of the recipe loaned itself to easy adaptation. In her *Kentucky Receipt Book*, Mary Harris Frazer added dried fruit and candied peel to her English Pound Cake:

> *One pound granulated sugar, sifted, 1 pound white butter, 1 ¼ pounds flour, 1 pound currants, 2 ounces of candied peel, ½ ounce citron, ½ ounce sweet almonds, 9 eggs. Cream butter, add sugar, then yolks beaten light, flour citron and peel; cut in thin slices, almonds blanched and chopped, currants washed and dried, fruit must be floured, using some of the same, 1 wine glass brandy or sherry wine, then beaten whites. Mix well, put in cake mold lined with buttered paper, bake more than 2 hours, have good heat in oven at beginning to prevent fruit sinking to the bottom. Cool a little before removing from the mold.*

This recipe, like many others, dates before the introduction of leavening agents. Air was incorporated into the mix via vigorous beating; the early English cookbook author Hannah Glasse instructed that it should be beaten "for an hour with your hand, or a great wooden spoon." Once baking powder became commonplace in recipes, the ratios of ingredients often changed.

A twentieth-century recipe for "Old Fashioned" pound cake, such as that in Kentucky Hospitality, is very different from those early recipes. Not only is baking powder now included, but milk is as well. Furthermore, measures are more likely to be done by volume as opposed to weight. The addition of baking powder makes the modern pound cake much lighter than its siblings from two centuries ago.

Old Fashioned Pound Cake
(as in Kentucky Hospitality)

1 cup butter
2 cups sugar
3 eggs
3 cups flour
2 teaspoons baking powder
1 cup milk
2 teaspoons vanilla extract
1 teaspoon almond extract

Cream the butter; add sugar gradually, beating at least 10 minutes. Add eggs, one at a time, beating thoroughly after each addition. Sift flour; measure and sift again. Mix ½ cup flour with baking powder and set aside. Add remaining flour to creamed mixture alternately with the milk. Add flavorings. Sift reserved flour over batter and stir, do not beat, until smooth. Pour into a well-greased and floured tube pan. Bake at 325° F for 1 hour or until golden brown.

According to eastern Kentucky and Appalachian lore, the stack cake was once a traditional wedding cake. People would bring a layer to the wedding, and they would be stacked with layers of apple butter sandwiched between them. The cakes were typically eight to twelve layers thick; some even speak of having seen sixteen-layer cakes—the more layers, the more beloved the bride in the community.

It's a charmingly romantic story, but as anyone who has made a stack cake knows, this is not something that you simply throw together at the last minute. It takes at least a day, closer to two, to sit and meld and for the apples to moisten the layers, so if it was a wedding cake, there must have been some serious forethought back in the mountains. On the other hand, it is possible that the wedding version used a more traditional sponge, as I have seen in occasional photos. One woman, as quoted by John and Anne van Willigen, described the stack cake her grandmother made, and it sounds somewhat different and requiring much less time:

> [It's] *really just a cake…She made* [the cake] *out of molasses…and put the dried apples between* [the layers]…*The cake'd be tall. With the thick slices instead of the thins that they make now…She'd make 'em one whole evenin'.*

Western Kentucky was a popular site for farming strawberries, as seen in this 1916 photo. *Lewis Wickes Hine, Library of Congress.*

This version would have required an oven, whereas the more common one described next needed little more than a skillet and a fire.

According to historian Sidney Saylor Farr, the recipe for the stack cake first made its way across the Cumberland Gap with the pioneer James Harrod, founder of Harrodsburg. The cake remains a mountain favorite to this day and makes the most of a Kentucky harvest, using dried apples and sorghum molasses. Unlike traditional sponge cakes, this is made with layers of stiff dough that slowly absorb the moisture of the apple filling.

Dried Apple Stack Cake (as Adapted from Mark Sohn's Recipe)

The cake is filled with a sort of jam or butter made from reconstituting the dried apples.

FILLING

6 cups dried apples*	1 teaspoon ginger
4 cups apple cider	1 teaspoon nutmeg
1 cup sugar	

*home-dried ones will not only hold up better than store-bought ones, but they will also have a much more concentrated flavor

Put the dried apples, cider and sugar in a large pot. Bring to a boil and then lower the heat to simmer for at least 30 minutes. Mix in the spices and then use a blender to blend it down to an applesauce consistency. Leave the mix to cool. If you prefer to keep larger apple chunks in your spread, by all means skip the blending step.

The next day, make the layers. The following is enough for six layers:

5 cups all-purpose flour
½ cup sugar
2 teaspoons baking powder
2 teaspoons ginger
1 teaspoon cinnamon
1 teaspoon salt
1 cup melted butter
1 cup sorghum
2 teaspoons vanilla
2 eggs

If you want to be ultra-traditional, you can use iron skillets. If not, use 9-inch cake tins.

Preheat the oven to 350° F. Put all of the dry ingredients into a large bowl and stir together. Make a well in the center of the bowl. Into the well pour the melted butter, the sorghum, vanilla and eggs. Start mixing, and soon you will be able to use your hands to mix everything into a dough. You might need to add a little more flour or water to get the right consistency.

Now take your lump of dough and roll it into a thick log. Cut the log into six equal parts. Each part will be one layer. Bake the layers for about 12 minutes. Once they have cooled, you are ready to assemble your cake.

Put the first layer on your cake plate and spread with ¾ cup of the apple mix. Repeat, alternating layers of cake and layers of apples, finishing with the sixth cake layer. Be careful when you are moving the cake at this point, as it is deceptively heavy. Leave the cake on the stand for about 10–12 hours at room temperature so the layers of cake can start to absorb the moisture from the apples. You can serve it now if you want to, but I strongly advise against it, as will any stack cake connoisseur. Resist a little longer and put your cake in the fridge for another 12–36 hours.

Finally, you are ready to serve the long-awaited cake. I dust mine with a little powdered sugar and make a basic cinnamon and vanilla glaze to pour over each slice. Other serving ideas include whipped cream, or you could warm the slices in the oven and top with ice cream.

Go to any family reunion or bake sale, and jam cake is sure to be somewhere among the offerings. Although usually referred to as Southern Jam Cake, this spicy concoction is best known in Kentucky; in fact, many people I've spoken to in other states farther south have never come across it. Little is known of its origins, but it remains a popular favorite. A mixture of spices, nuts and jam, the cake may be topped with cream cheese frosting or, as in this recipe, a caramel drizzle.

The following jam cake recipe has been handed down in my husband's family and comes with a possible link to the criminal underworld. Young married couple Printus and Fronia Duncan decided that they would travel to the Windy City in search of work during the Prohibition era. Once there, they paid a service to find employment among the city's wealthier clientele. Fronia was hired as a house cleaner and cook, and Printus found a job as a cook…at one of the many establishments operated by gangster Al Capone. (For Capone's other connection to Kentucky, read about the Hot Brown in Part VI). They quickly realized that those who worked in Capone's businesses had a tendency to disappear; they were, after all, constantly overhearing the mob's dealings. Fearful of Capone's illicit activities and what might happen to them, the Duncans decided to move back to Kentucky, to Fronia's hometown of Manchester. Having access through the kitchens to Capone's stash of bootleg Canadian whiskey, they began to secretly sell some to raise enough money to buy bus tickets home. The couple lived out the rest of their days in Manchester, Printus always keeping one eye open, for fear that he would be found.

But what of the cake? Printus Duncan claimed that he had made his jam cake recipe when employed as a cook and that Al Capone was particularly fond of a slice. Once settled back in Clay County, Fronia worked for my husband's grandmother for many years, having known her as a child. One year, she made the jam cake, and it met with such praise that people begged her to share the recipe. The jam cake became a feature of many family events, and although we shall never know whether Mr. Capone really did enjoy a piece of the luscious baked good, it has earned the nickname "Mafia Cake."

"Mafia" Jam Cake

1 cup butter, softened
1½ cups sugar
5 eggs
3 cups flour
1½ teaspoons allspice
1 teaspoon cinnamon
¼ teaspoon salt
1 teaspoon baking soda
1 cup buttermilk
1 cup pecans, chopped
2 cups jam (seedless is best)

FOR CARAMEL FROSTING:
1 stick butter
1 cup brown sugar
½ cup milk
2 cups powdered sugar

Preheat the oven to 325° F. Cream the butter and sugar together until light and fluffy. Add the well-beaten eggs. Sift the flour, spices and salt into a bowl. Dissolve the baking soda in the buttermilk. Add the buttermilk and the flour alternately to the egg, sugar and butter mixture, beating well after each addition. Dredge the nuts in a little flour and add to the cake mix along with the jam. Stir well. Pour into greased and floured tube pan. Bake for 60 minutes. Cool on a wire rack.

For the frosting, bring the butter and brown sugar to a boil. Cook for 2 minutes, stirring constantly. Add the milk and return to the boil. Remove pan from heat and add the powdered sugar. Stir until it starts to thicken and drizzle over the cooled cake.

Bible Cake

Also know as Scripture Cake, this appears to have originated in the British Isles during the eighteenth century. Each ingredient is linked to a verse in the Bible, and therefore, to fully grasp the recipe, one would need to know his scriptures, a useful teaching tool no doubt. The verses differ from one recipe to the next, although the ingredients remain the same. This version even gives the instructions for making the cake as a biblical reference.

3½ cups flour (1 Kings 4:22)
1 cup butter (Judges 5:25)
1½ cups sugar (Jeremiah 6:20)
2 cups raisins (1 Samuel 30:12)
2 cups figs (Isaiah 38:21)
1 cup water (Genesis 24:17)
1 cup almonds (Number 17:8)
6 eggs (Isaiah 10:14)
1 teaspoon honey (Exodus 16:31)
pinch of salt (Leviticus 2:13)
2 teaspoons baking powder (1 Corinthians 5:6)
1 teaspoon each cinnamon and nutmeg (II Chronicles 9:9)

To make the cake, follow Solomon's advice for disciplining a child in Proverbs 23:14. Mix everything, pour into a greased cake tin and bake for 1 hour at 350° F.

Coca-Cola Cake

2 cups flour
2 cups sugar
3 sticks butter
6 tablespoons cocoa powder
1 cup Coca-Cola, plus an extra 6 tablespoons
1½ cups buttermilk
1 teaspoon baking soda
2 eggs
1 teaspoon vanilla
1½ cups mini marshmallows
16 ounces powdered sugar

Combine the flour and sugar. In a pan, melt the butter over a low heat. Add 3 tablespoons cocoa powder and 1 cup cola. Bring to a boil and then pour the liquid over the flour. Add the buttermilk, baking soda, eggs, vanilla extract and marshmallows and mix well. Pour into a greased baking pan and bake for 35 minutes at 350° F.

Allow the cake to cool but only for about 15 minutes before frosting. To make the frosting, mix the powdered sugar with the remaining cocoa powder and cola. Spread over the still-warm cake.

It would be a grave error to write a chapter about Kentucky and cakes without including some mention of Duncan Hines, the man whose name is now synonymous with commercial cake mixes. Unlike so many food characters, Duncan Hines was a real person. Born in 1880 in Bowling Green, Kentucky, he attended the Bowling Green Business University for a few years before heading west; as an asthmatic, he hoped that the dried climate would be beneficial. Hines spent several decades as a traveling salesman, working on behalf of a Chicago print company. As he traveled, he took detailed notes of every restaurant and diner that he visited. After all, this was the era before interstates and chain restaurants, when the mom and pop diner thrived. He eventually put the notes together into a series of books, the first of which was *Adventures in Good Eating*, published in 1936. The notes were brief but detailed, offering restaurant locations, hours, pricing information and a summary of the menu. This was an era when there were no health inspections; travelers would have found the trustworthy guidebook invaluable. *Adventures in Good Eating* proved so popular that Duncan and his wife, Florence, followed it up with a 1938 book of lodging recommendations and, eventually, a regular nationally syndicated newspaper column, offering make-at-home adaptations of favorite restaurant dishes. Meanwhile, restaurants and motels clamored to earn the right to display one of his "Recommended by Duncan Hines" signs.

Sadly, Florence Hines died in 1938, an event that led to Duncan giving up life on the road and returning to his native Kentucky. Ever cautious, he was careful not to lend his name to anything that might compromise his reputation, despite the numerous offers he received. In 1948, Hines sold the rights to his name and his books to Roy Park, and Hines-Park Foods was born, with the intention of improving America's eating. By 1952, Duncan Hines was a recognized name on dozens of food products. The first Duncan Hines cake mixes were developed and quickly captured a sizable share of the domestic baking market. In 1956, Hines-Park was sold to Procter & Gamble. Hines passed away in 1959, his death caused by lung cancer. The guidebooks published in his name ceased in 1962, but the man remains known as the name behind the cake mixes.

This being Kentucky, there is, of course, an annual Duncan Hines Festival, honoring the man, raising money for local charities and hosting the Adventures in Good Baking Contest.

DESSERTS

There's no denying that Southerners, and that includes Kentuckians, have a sweet tooth. In addition to sweet tea, it's not uncommon to find a range of available desserts at a meal: jam cakes, fried apple pies, cream pies, chess pies, peanut butter pie…the list is endless.

The first time I was asked if I "would like some nog," I was at a loss for how to respond. Was this some bizarre Kentucky Christmas tradition that I was not familiar with? To make matters worse, I was then offered custard. Having grown up with instant custard for school lunches, formed from adding boiling water to powder to create a yellow, usually lumpy goo, I was even more lost. Why on earth would I want some of that? Oh, how I had lost touch with the English traditions of yesteryear.

Both eggnog (the nog in question) and boiled custard are Christmas favorites at many Kentucky homes, and they both have their origins in ancient Rome and England, it would seem. John Egerton suspects that eggnog and custard were once the same dish but that they became distinct in the Victorian era, one taking on an alcoholic addition (although as you can see from the recipes here, *The Kentucky Housewife* author Mrs Lettice Bryan enjoyed a touch of liquor in either dish). Depending on its thickness, boiled custard may be either a sipping beverage or a rich dessert. And while eggnog once used only egg yolks, some folks follow what was believed to be George Washington's recipe and throw in the egg whites too. However you make them and whether you choose to sip or spoon the custard, both now hold pride of place at the festive Kentucky table.

Lettice Bryan's Eggnog

6 egg yolks
1 quart of thick cream
7 tablespoons sugar
nutmeg to taste
7 wine glasses of preferred liquor

Beat the egg yolks lightly into the cream and add the sugar and nutmeg. Pour over the liquor and allow to stand for an hour.

Lettice Bryan's Custard Sauce

1 pint milk
2 eggs, beaten
1 cup of sugar
brandy or wine, to taste

Heat milk to boiling point. Gradually add the beaten eggs, sugar and brandy or wine and put over a second pan of hot water to cook until it has reached a good consistency.

Ask what a traditional Kentuckian dessert might be, and banana pudding will probably be mentioned, which is odd since bananas are most certainly not grown here. Yet Kentucky and bananas have a fascinating historical relationship, and it's largely due to a little town in the western part of the state by the name of Fulton. Although bananas had been an imported favorite since America's colonial days, the railroads made them more widely available. During the 1800s, there were numerous attempts to make a refrigerated railroad car that would allow for the transportation of fruits and other perishable goods across the country. In 1875, Georgia farmer Samuel Rumph successfully invented one and was then able to ship his fresh peaches to markets in other states.

Five years later, the Illinois Central Railroad introduced a refrigerated car to carry bananas from New Orleans to the north and Midwest. Fulton, and its partner town just across the Tennessee line, South Fulton, happened to be the site for a railroad switch point and major distribution center for all fruit shipped from New Orleans. Fulton soon became known as the "Banana Crossroads of America." With the arrival of the interstate system and trucking as a major method of transportation, the need for railroads declined. By the 1950s, Fulton's banana heyday was gone, and this part of the town's history risked being forgotten. So, the town did what all ingenious southern towns do in such circumstances: it held a festival to commemorate its past importance. In 1962, the first International Banana Festival was held in the perhaps unlikely (to those unfamiliar with the history) spot of Fulton, Kentucky. The festival celebrates the history of agriculture and transportation in both Fulton and its Tennessee counterpart and attracts dignitaries from banana-growing nations in Latin America among its thousands of visitors. Crafts, both local and Latin American, are also available, but perhaps the biggest attraction of the event is the one-ton banana pudding. Should you feel so inclined to make your own at home, you will need three thousand bananas and someone to peel them all.

Martha McCulloch-Williams was an avid fan of the banana: "They can be cooked in fifty ways—and in each be found excellent." However, the first recipe for banana pudding seems to be that given by Mary Harris Frazer:

> Take ½ dozen bananas, peel and cut in pieces an inch thick, put in baking dish and pour over custard made in the following manner: Custard—One pint of milk, 3 eggs, beat the yolks light, add milk, also 2 tablespoons of granulated sugar. Have the milk boiling, add the eggs and let it cook until it thickens; when cool pour over the bananas. Make a meringue with whites of the eggs and granulated sugar, put on top of custard, set in oven a few minutes to brown. Serve at once.

The banana pudding is rather reminiscent of the English trifle, with its layers of rich banana custard and cream. Nilla Wafers later became considered an essential addition to the banana pudding, and the meringue occasionally gives way to whipped cream.

Banana Pudding

This pudding may be served with a topping of either meringue or whipped cream.

4 cups Nilla Wafers	2⅓ cups milk
5 bananas, sliced	3 egg yolks
½ cup, plus 1 tablespoon sugar	2 tablespoons butter
⅓ cup flour	2 teaspoons vanilla extract

Place 2 cups of wafers in the bottom of a dish. Put half of the bananas in a layer on top of the wafers. Repeat with the remaining wafers and banana slices.

Combine the sugar and flour in a bowl. Heat the milk in a saucepan but do not bring to a boil. Slowly whisk the sugar and flour into the milk and then whisk in the egg yolks. Continue to cook over a medium heat, stirring all the while until you have a thick custard. Stir in the butter and the vanilla extract. Pour in the dish over the wafers and bananas.

Allow to stand at room temperature for 20 minutes and then place in the refrigerator. Once chilled, cover to prevent skin from forming and refrigerate overnight.

Coconut Cream Pie

Bananas and coconuts. Kentuckians love their sweets and have a skill at making nonnative ingredients into traditional dishes that are definitely regional in their followings. This is a twist on the original custard cream pie.

1 cup flaked coconut
¾ cup sugar
3 egg yolks
1½ cups coconut milk
½ cup heavy cream
⅓ cup cornstarch
1 teaspoon vanilla extract
1 pie shell
whipped cream and more coconut, for the topping

Toast the flaked coconut for a few minutes until lightly browned. In a pan, mix the sugar, egg yolks, coconut milk, cream and cornstarch. Stir constantly as you bring to a boil over a low heat. Remove the pan from the heat and stir in the coconut and the vanilla extract. Pour the mixture into the pie shell. Refrigerate for about 4 hours until firm. Top with whipped cream and more toasted coconut.

Chess Pie

No one knows how chess pie really got its name. Many food historians agree that it is an Americanization of cheese pie, an old English pie that used lemon curd (also known as lemon cheese) as a filling. Some say that the dessert is so sweet that it was called chest pie, in reference to the pie chests where it could be kept much longer than other pies, and over time "chest" became "chess." One more unusual explanation I have come across is that southern gentlemen would retire to play chess…with a slice of pie. Bourbon and a cigar sound much more likely in that scenario. And then there's the claim that the name is from dialect: "It's jes' pie (just pie)." The ingredients are the standards that appear in many a Kentucky dessert—the standards that just about any housewife has on hand: eggs, butter, flour (some recipes use cornmeal) and sugar. Lots of sugar.

Mary Randolph has a recipe in *The Virginia Housewife* for a Transparent Pudding, which is, for all intents and purposes, the same recipe as a modern chess pie:

Beat eight eggs very light, add half a pound of pounded sugar, the same of fresh butter melted, and half a nutmeg grated; sit it on a stove and keep stirring till it is as thick as buttered eggs—put a puff paste in a shallow dish, pour in the ingredients, and bake it half an hour in a moderate oven; sift sugar over it, and serve it up hot.

Nevertheless, the actual name "chess pie" rarely appears in any of the old cookbooks; the first instance I have come across is in Estelle Woods Wilcox's 1877 *Buckeye Cookery and Practical Housekeeping*. She shared a recipe from a Miss Carson of Glendale for chess pie:

Three eggs, two-thirds cup sugar, half cup butter (half cup milk may be added if not wanted so rich); beat butter to a cream, then add yolks and sugar beaten to a froth with the flavoring; stir all together rapidly, and bake in a nice crust. When done, spread with the beaten whites, and three table-spoons sugar and a little flavoring. Return to oven and brown slightly. This makes one pie, which should be served immediately.

The flavoring to which Miss Glendale refers is probably vanilla extract and/or nutmeg, both of which are common additions. However, there is now a number of flavored chess pies, from lemon to chocolate. One popular variation of the chess pie is the Kentucky Pie, better known to many as the Jefferson Davis Pie. Kentucky being the true border state during the Civil War, it was the birthplace of the presidents of both the Union and the Confederacy. Jefferson Davis was born in Christian County, and although his family moved farther south to Mississippi during his childhood, he returned to Lexington's Transylvania University for his studies. We shall probably never know if Davis ever really ate this pie; some say it is a traditional Davis family recipe, while others say the name is pure coincidence and that it was really created in Missouri. Here in Kentucky, we choose to believe the former.

Jefferson Davis Pie

1 cup white sugar
1 cup brown sugar
1 tablespoon flour
¼ teaspoon nutmeg
¼ teaspoon cinnamon
1 cup heavy cream
4 eggs, lightly beaten
½ cup butter, melted
1 tablespoon lemon juice
1 teaspoon lemon zest
pinch of salt
1 teaspoon vanilla
1 unbaked pie shell

Mix the sugars, flour, nutmeg and cinnamon in a bowl. Pour in the cream and stir. Add the eggs and whisk the mix together. Finally, add the butter, lemon juice, lemon zest, salt and vanilla and mix again until well combined. Pour into the pie shell. Bake in a 400° F oven for 10 minutes. Then lower the heat to 350° F and bake for a further 45 minutes. Serve with whipped cream.

Chocolate-Nut Pie

¾ cup semisweet chocolate chips
1 cup walnuts, chopped
1 8-inch pie crust
½ cup butter, melted
¾ cup white sugar
½ cup all-purpose flour
2 eggs
1 tablespoon bourbon

Preheat oven to 350° F (175° C). Spread chocolate chips and nuts in bottom of pie shell. In a mixing bowl, cream butter or margarine and sugar together. Mix in flour. Beat the eggs slightly and mix into the creamed mixture. Stir in bourbon. Pour filling into pie shell (over chips and nuts). Bake for 30 to 40 minutes.

CANDIES

Kentuckians love their candies and sweet treats, and history shows that they've been quick to try out the candy-making potential of ingredients from bourbon to corn syrup to potatoes.

Colonial Americans enjoyed candies made from sugar, maple syrup and nuts. Many recipes began as medicinal lozenges, for example peppermints and hard-boiled candies. Native Americans and white settlers alike enjoyed spun taffy made from maple syrup, made in the same was as the pulled sorghum mentioned earlier. One might also expect to find marzipan fruits, sugar plums and various candied items.

A notable Kentucky confectioner of the nineteenth century was Monsieur Mathurin Giron, a five-foot-tall Frenchman who moved to Lexington, married the daughter of a wealthy French immigrant in Bourbon County and opened a store on Mill Street. A lively storyteller, M. Giron claimed to have been a member of Napoleon's guard and to have traveled throughout Europe. He is first listed in Lexington's directory in 1811, but his business making cakes and candies would prosper until his retirement in 1844. In 1833, he added a dancing school above his confectionery. The young Mary Todd attended many of the balls held at the location. While known at the time for his fine candies and chocolates, Giron's lasting legacy to Kentucky food has been a cake.

In 1825, Fayette County namesake the Marquis de Lafayette paid a visit to the United States, and he included Lexington in his tour. To commemorate the occasion and his fellow Frenchman, M. Giron baked an elaborate cake for the Masonic banquet held in Lafayette's honor. The cake was well received. The story goes that the cake was so impressive that Lafayette refused to cut a piece, instead keeping it whole so that he might admire it the following day. Giron later shared the recipe with the Todd family. It was said to have become a family favorite. Mary, in particular, enjoyed making this cake, and Abraham Lincoln enjoyed singing the praises of Mary's wonderful white cake. Despite its origin, the cake has become forever associated with the president. Note the inclusion of baking powder, which was not introduced until 1849 or thereabouts and would not be used regularly for several decades more. If the recipe is indeed genuine, the addition of baking powder would have been a later alteration to the recipe.

The Lincoln Cake

2 cups sugar
1 cup butter
3 cups flour
1 tablespoon baking powder
1 cup milk
1 cup almonds, blanched and chopped
1½ teaspoons vanilla extract
6 egg whites, with ½ teaspoon salt

Preheat oven to 350° F. Cream together the sugar and butter. Sift together flour and baking powder three times; slowly add to the butter and sugar mixture alternately with milk, in small amounts at a time. Mix thoroughly. Add the chopped, blanched almonds and vanilla to the mixture. Continue beating until thoroughly mixed. In a separate bowl, stiffly beat egg whites with salt. Gently fold them into the first mixture. Pour the mixture into a greased and floured angel food cake pan or Bundt pan. Bake for 1 hour or until a toothpick inserted into the center comes out clean. Allow the cake to cool for a few minutes until you are able to gently remove it from the pan. Before serving, gently cut the cake with a serrated bread or cake knife to avoid tearing it.

The cake may be served as is or with frosting. Marion Flexner included a recipe for a frosting so delicate and southern that I can instantly visualize Mary Todd making it to make the cake extra special for her Abe.

Lincoln Cake Frosting

2 cups sugar
2 egg whites, beaten with a pinch of salt
½ cup candied pineapple, diced
1 cup water
1 teaspoon vanilla
½ cup crystallized cherries, cut in half

Boil the sugar and water until the syrup spins a 5-inch thread. Fold slowly into the well-beaten egg whites, adding 1 tablespoon at a time until 4 have been added. Now add the remaining syrup in its entirety, pouring slowly. Beat hard until the mixture stands in stiff peaks. Just before spreading on the cake, add the vanilla and fold in the pineapple and cherries.

In seeking more information about the Lincoln Cake, I also came across the following recipe, dated 1865, in *Civil War Recipes: Receipts from the Pages of Godey's Lady's Book*. Sadly, no further information is given beyond the ingredients.

Lincoln Cake

Two eggs, two cups of sugar, a half cup of butter, one of sweet milk, three of flour, one teaspoonful of cream or tartar, half a teaspoonful of soda, and one of lemon essence.

The Industrial Revolution brought new possibilities in candy-making. Chocolate arrived on the scene, forever changing the world of sweets. Specialized confectioners gave way to mass-produced penny candies.

In the early years of the twentieth century, corn syrup was gaining popularity in the market, and many were keen to try this sugar substitute. One candy that surfaced around that time was Divinity. Considered to be typically southern, little is known of its true origins—who invented it, how it was named and so on. The most common story is that the name comes from someone tasting it and declaring that it was quite divine. Success in making divinity candy is reliant on the weather—too humid and the mixture cannot dry.

Many candy companies began in Kentucky kitchens, where women would make a batch of something sweet, perhaps to share with their friends or to serve at a social occasion. People enjoyed them and asked to buy some, and soon there was enough demand to open fully-fledged businesses. One such case is Rebecca-Ruth Candy, based in Frankfort. Not only is this a story of candy, but it is also the story of two women operating a business at a time when doing so was almost unheard of. It was 1919, and Ruth Hanly and Rebecca Gooch were substitute teachers, one of the few professions open to women in those days. Sadly, teaching is a calling, and both women realized that they did not enjoy it—nor were they very good at it. Luckily, they had something to fall back on. You see, both women enjoyed making chocolate. Each year, they made chocolate as gifts for friends and family, always receiving high praise for their work. But this was an era when even the few women who did go into business for themselves usually did so with the financial backing of a husband. Ruth and Rebecca were both single and determined that they did not need husbands to provide for them. Together, they decided to forge a business partnership. Rebecca-Ruth Candy was born. It was a decision that would earn them strong support from some quarters and equally strong ridicule from others.

The women rented the barroom at the Frankfort Hotel; since Prohibition had gone into effect, the bar was not seeing much use. To promote their new wares, they relied on word of mouth from those who had tried them, as well as their own gumption in getting out to tell people about these wonderful new chocolates that they had recently come across. According to company history, it was not unusual for one of them to approach a complete stranger on the street to sing the praises of Rebecca Ruth.

In the late 1920s, the partnership between the two entrepreneurs took a few twists and turns. In 1924, Ruth married World War I veteran Douglas Booe, and they moved to northern Kentucky. She continued to make candies, but it is unclear whether this was still as part of Rebecca-Ruth. Just eight months after giving birth to a son, John, in 1927, Ruth suddenly found herself widowed. Her husband had been wounded in the war and had been in weak health ever since. Now a young widow with a baby to support, she moved back to Frankfort.

Two years later, it was Rebecca's turn to get married, a move that led to her selling her share of the business. Ruth was now the sole owner of Rebecca-Ruth—running a business, single-parenting a child and about to enter the Great Depression. The stock market crash of 1929 sent a tidal wave of crises across the entire nation. Millions of people lost their jobs and their homes and were plunged into poverty. Who could afford such trivial luxuries as chocolates? The previously thriving mail-order business dived. When people did have some spare change to buy chocolate, it was now just one piece at a time. Already no stranger to adversity, Ruth used the time to experiment with creating new candies, confident that this was but a temporary ripple in her fortunes. Further tragedy struck in 1933 when fire destroyed her home, as well as all of her candy-making equipment. Ruth and the infant, John, were left with nothing but the same marble slab that she and Rebecca had first used back in the Frankfort Hotel. Still undaunted, Ruth decided that it was time to approach the bank for a loan. After all, she had been running a successful business until the Depression. However, the banks were in no mood to make loans. She was refused by every one.

Rebecca-Ruth Candy was a company started by the determined efforts of two women, and so perhaps it is only fitting that the kindness of another woman was the factor that prevented the name Rebecca Ruth from disappearing into the mists of time. Fanny Rump, a local hotel housekeeper, agreed to loan Ruth the sum of fifty dollars to rebuild her business. Ruth's most famous creation also arose from the suggestion of another woman. Eleanor Hume Offutt got to talking with Ruth as Frankfort celebrated its 150th birthday. Conversation naturally turned to sweets, and Ms. Offutt mentioned how wonderful it would be if there were a chocolate that incorporated Kentucky bourbon. For the next two years, Ruth worked to find just the right formula, and in 1938, she unveiled the Bourbon Ball. It was an instant hit. By the time World War II rolled around, even rationing could not stop Rebecca Ruth. Loyal customers saved their sugar rations to share with Ruth.

In 1964, Ruth Hanly Booe retired from a life of entrepreneurship, handing the reins of the company to her son, John. He further expanded the business, growing the mail-order and wholesale divisions and, following in his mother's footsteps, creating new liquor-filled chocolates. Although he sold the business to his son, Charles, in 1997, he remained active at Rebecca Ruth until his death in 2012. Today, Rebecca-Ruth Candy continues to operate out of Frankfort and is as successful as ever, a lasting legacy to the dreams and determination of two young Kentucky women who dared to do what others said they could not.

Another woman who started her candy-making business at about the same time as Ruth Hanly and Rebecca Gooch was Ruth Tharpe Hunt of Mount Sterling. Like the founders of Rebecca-Ruth, Hunt began by making candies for friends but frequently received requests for more. In 1921, she set up shop in her home, but by 1930, her business, Ruth Hunt Candy Company, had grown to the point that it needed its own location. The factory moved to an even larger facility in 2001. It is still in operation today, and visitors can view the original marble slabs and copper kettles. Ruth Hunt's most famous candy is the Blue Monday. Legend has it that she created it after a salesman mentioned that he always enjoyed a little something sweet "to help me through my blue Monday." The resulting bar is a rich cream candy covered in chocolate—perfect for those blue Mondays.

Potato Candy

In a move that would make their Irish ancestors proud, Kentuckians have found another use for the potato. When mixed with sugar and peanut butter, it makes a candy that is still enjoyed by many today.

1 boiled potato
powdered sugar (as much as 2 pounds might be needed for one potato)
peanut butter

Peel the boiled potato while still warm and mash it in a bowl. Stir in powdered sugar until you have a dough. Don't let the potato cool at this point, as it will become hard and you will be unable to make the starchy dough that you need. Once you have a thick dough, roll it out to a quarter inch thickness on a surface covered with more powdered sugar. Spread a layer of peanut butter over the rolled-out dough. Now roll the dough like a jelly roll. Allow it to harden in the refrigerator for an hour or so before cutting into slices.

Bourbon Balls

1 cup pecans, finely chopped
5 tablespoons good-quality bourbon
½ cup butter, soft
16 ounces powdered sugar
chocolate, for coating
pecan halves, for topping

Soak the chopped nuts in the bourbon overnight. The next day, mix them with the butter and powdered sugar. Form into balls and refrigerate overnight. When set, dip in melted chocolate to coat and top with a pecan half.

Divinity

There are many variations to this recipe, with some adding food coloring, omitting the chopped nuts or dipping in chocolate.

2 cups sugar
½ cup corn syrup
½ cup water
2 egg whites
1 teaspoon vanilla extract
1 teaspoon powdered sugar
½ cup chopped pecans

In a pan, bring the sugar, corn syrup and water to a boil and stir until all the sugar has dissolved. Using a candy thermometer, cook until the mixture has reached 260° F. Beat the egg whites until they form stiff peaks. Slowly pour the hot syrup into the egg whites, beating all the while. Add the vanilla, powdered sugar and nuts and continue to beat until the mixture holds its shape. Drop teaspoonfuls onto waxed paper and leave to firm.

PART VI
KENTUCKY SPECIALTIES

The Hot Brown (as Provided by the Brown Hotel)

The Roaring Twenties. The age of jazz, gangsters and flappers. While the glamour of the era may have skipped much of Kentucky, Louisville attracted its fair share of the criminal and literary elite. Al Capone and F. Scott Fitzgerald were frequent visitors, the latter using the city's Seelbach Hotel in his novel *The Great Gatsby*. Louisville's movers and shakers knew the hot spots for drinking, dancing and gambling, and it was in this party-filled society that one of Kentucky's most beloved dishes was created.

The Brown Hotel held nightly dinner dances, each event attracting well over one thousand guests, many of them carousing into the early hours. Needing a little sustenance after a prolonged evening of revelry, the guests would request a hearty dish of bacon and eggs from the Brown's head chef Fred Schmidt. After a while, they were bored by the same meal, and so, one night some of them issued him a challenge to create something new. Using the ingredients at hand—ham, turkey, bread and cheese—Schmidt created an open-faced sandwich that became known as the Hot Brown. The dish proved popular, and soon the Hot Brown (and its cold cousin) were featured on the hotel's menu, becoming part of Louisville's culinary history.

The Hot Brown has undergone a few minor tweaks since its inception; it is said that pimentos were on the original sandwich, but these have now been replaced by sliced tomatoes. Pecorino Romano or cheddar is sometimes used

Louisville's Brown Hotel was the source of the beloved Hot Brown. *The Brown Hotel.*

123

The crowded tearooms at the Brown Hotel. *J. Grahams.*

instead of the original Parmesan. Otherwise, the recipe remains unchanged. Its popularity also means that you can find it on menus throughout Louisville and indeed throughout Kentucky. Meanwhile, the Brown Hotel estimates that it has sold more than 1.7 million Hot Browns since that evening in 1926 when Chef Schmidt threw a few things together for his guests. The following makes two sandwiches.

2 ounces butter
2 ounces flour
16 ounces cream
½ cup Pecorino Romano cheese
salt and pepper
2 slices Texas toast or thick white bread, toasted
14 ounces sliced turkey
2 tomatoes, sliced in half
4 slices crispy cooked bacon

Prepare a roux by melting the butter in a pan and stirring in the flour until you have a thick paste. Cook over a low heat for 2 minutes, stirring constantly so that the roux does not burn. Add the cream and whisk lightly as you bring the mixture to a simmer. Remove the pan from the heat and add the cheese, stirring until melted. Add salt and pepper to taste.

Place the pieces of toast in individual ovenproof dishes and cover the bread with the turkey. Add the tomato slices. Then pour the sauce over the sandwich. Sprinkle on a little extra cheese at this point.

Broil until the cheese has browned. Place two slices of bacon on top in a cross and enjoy while it's hot. This is, after all, a Hot Brown!

Derby Pie

Kentuckians are protective of their local dishes and establishments, none more so than Kern's Kitchen, makers of the famed Derby Pie®. There are many chocolate nut pies, but call them a Derby Pie® and you face a sharp slap on the wrist. The only true Derby Pie® was created by Walter and

Leaudra Kern sets the company's Derby Pies® to cool. *Kern's Kitchen.*

Leaudra Kern and their son, George, more than fifty years ago. George was manager of the Prospect Inn in Melrose and turned to his parents for help with creating a new dessert option. To choose the name for the new creation, each family member put an idea in a hat. The name drawn was the one that is now trademarked. Five decades on, the family continues to make this best-selling pie, available at many restaurants and stores throughout the area. The recipe remains a closely guarded secret; all that is known is that it contains chocolate chips and walnut pieces…and is delicious.

Goetta

In the northern Kentucky area, just across the river from Cincinnati, there is a food so popular that it has inspired two annual festivals. Goetta is an enduring testament to the culinary contributions of the region's German population.

The first landowner in what is now Kenton County was technically a German. Gerhard Muse of Hannover had fought against the French in the 1754 war with the promise of land as payment. Sure enough, in 1763, a king's proclamation granted him two hundred acres along the banks of the Ohio River. It seems many did not hold the king's word in high regard in those days. Having only looked at a map and never visited the land, Muse traded it for a keg of brandy. The parcel was traded several more times, for meat and other commodities. Not until 1792 was the land finally settled. Given its convenient location en route between Lexington and Cincinnati, a ferry service began, and a town sprung up. Covington was named after the Anglicized version of a general of German descent. The town grew slowly, attracting a few German settlers. Although few in number, they formed a tight-knit cultural community. Numbers would later grow, and today there is a clear German influence in Covington, especially in the Mainstrasse German village area. It is here that one of the annual goetta festivals takes place.

The German love for sausage is widely known, and goetta developed as an immigrant twist on traditional dishes from the homeland, based on what was locally available. Goetta is a combination of ground pork, beef, onions, spices and steelcut oats, with the oats acting as a filler, stretching the meat supply a little further. It is most commonly served like a breakfast sausage. German Americans made their own goetta until one local butcher, Robert Glier, had the idea of commercializing his recipe in the 1940s. Today, Glier's Goetta is still the best-known brand.

Crockpot Goetta

5 cups water
1 tablespoon salt
1 teaspoon pepper
1 bay leaf
2½ cups steelcut oats
1 pound ground beef
1 pound ground pork shoulder
1 onion, chopped

Set crockpot temperature to high. Put the water, salt, pepper and bay leaf in cooker and bring to a boil. Add oats and cook for 90 minutes. Mix together the meats and the onion. Stir into the oat mixture. Switch the crockpot heat to low and cook for 3 hours. Remove the mixture from the crockpot and spread onto a baking tray lined with wax paper. Leave to cool and then chill for 1 hour until solid. Cut into slices and fry to serve.

Beer Cheese

From bars and diners to the finest award-winning restaurants, there's one thing that is sure to be on the menu throughout central Kentucky: beer cheese. Yet the combination of cheese, beer and spices remains relatively unknown to anyone outside the region.

The origins of beer cheese are hotly debated. Many historians believe that it originated in bars in the late nineteenth century. Not wanting to waste flat beer, barkeepers added it to cheese, creating a spicy dip that they could serve the following day.

Beer cheese bears a striking resemblance to several cheese dishes that would have been introduced by immigrants, including Welsh rarebit (or rabbit, depending which historian or cookbook you choose to follow). Rarebits (as I grew up knowing them in England) were a popular supper dish of gooey melted cheese on hot toast. Grated cheese was mixed with beer, mustard and spices and then spread on a thick slice of toasted bread before being placed back near a flame to melt. When properly prepared, the topping was golden and bubbly. It seems the Welsh rarebit was just one of many varieties of rarebit, all carried over to the colonies by immigrants from the British Isles; one English rarebit called for a glass of port wine to be poured over the toast as it cooked. Could beer cheese be a simpler adaptation of an old rarebit?

Perhaps it bears the strongest similarity to Obatzter, a cheese spread believed to have originated in the beer gardens of Bavaria. A soft cheese, such as Camembert, is mixed with butter, spices and beer, and the resulting Obatzter is served with pretzels. It is certainly plausible that German bartenders here in Kentucky substituted whatever cheese was available. On the other hand, there are those who claim that the original German recipe was invented by an innkeeper in the 1920s, leaving us to wonder which came first: the beer cheese or the Obatzter.

In 1949, Marion Flexner, author of *Out of Kentucky Kitchens*, wrote of the "days when free lunches were served with every 5-cent glass of beer." Beer cheese was a part of this lunch. Flexner had some trouble finding anyone who could remember the concoction, but eventually she found someone willing to share the recipe, which she termed "a perfect understudy for Welsh rabbit." Her suggestion that it had fallen into obscurity contradicts the claim of many modern beer cheese producers that every family had a recipe, passed down through generations.

Whatever the true origins of beer cheese, the savviest marketer was Johnnie Allman of Winchester. The owner of a small diner, Johnnie served his cousin Joe's "snappy cheese" in the 1940s. Joe had recently moved back to Kentucky from Phoenix, Arizona, and missed the spicy food. Allman's snappy cheese became so popular that to this day it is accepted as the original, despite evidence to the contrary. Johnnie Allman's diner is long gone, but his brand of beer cheese continues.

Today, beer cheese is big business in central Kentucky. There is even an annual festival devoted to the spicy cheese product. Since its debut in 2009, the Beer Cheese Festival has grown to attract more than ten thousand visitors. The highlight of the festival is its competition, with categories for both professional and amateur beer cheese makers. The 2012 amateur division winner Ollie Puckett's secret for a good beer cheese is to "whip, whip, whip." The pros advise keeping it simple: beer, cheese and spices.

Beer cheese can be used as a dip with crackers or carrots, as a spread or as a topping for burgers and hot dogs. Here is the basic recipe, but the taste can vary according to the cheese, beer and amount of spices you add. Most people use a cheddar-type cheese, but I've spoken to some who prefer to add some creamier cheese to aid with a smoother texture.

1 pound cheese, typically a sharp cheddar, at room temperature
½ cup flat beer
2 cloves garlic, minced
½ teaspoon cayenne pepper
½ teaspoon Tabasco sauce

Mix the ingredients together in a blender until it reaches the texture you desire. Add further seasoning if you prefer a spicier beer cheese. Keep refrigerated.

Benedictine

At the opposite, more genteel end of the spreadable cheese spectrum is Benedictine, the cucumber and cream cheese sandwich filling created by Louisville businesswoman Jennie Carter Benedict. A graduate of the Boston School of Cooking, she opened her first restaurant in 1893, followed by a tearoom in 1900. At the turn of the twentieth century and well into the 1920s, Miss Jennie operated several local tearooms, ran a catering business, edited a section of the local newspaper and published several cookbooks. It is said that she was offered $1 million to relocate to St. Louis in 1923, but public outcry in Louisville was such that she stayed put. Her famous Benedictine spread recalls an elegant time when ladies took afternoon tea.

8 ounces cream cheese
¼ cup mayonnaise
green food coloring (just the smallest amount—aim for a hint of green)
2 tablespoons finely grated onion
1 cucumber, peeled and seeded
a dash of Tabasco sauce or a sprinkling of cayenne pepper

Mix the cream cheese, mayonnaise, green food coloring and onion. Grate the cucumber into the cream cheese mixture and stir in. Season to taste with Tabasco. Transfer to a dish and serve with crackers or use as a filling in finger sandwiches.

Pool Hall Chili

A pool hall might not be the place you expect a food sensation to be born, but the chili bun is not your average food. Ronni Lundy described it as having been "born in sin…They have little redeeming social or nutritional value." Nevertheless, they are, as Lundy noted, "one of the best-tasting things you'll ever put in your mouth." Chili has its own regional qualities. In northern Kentucky and across the Ohio state line in Cincinnati, the dish is likely to come with a strong dose of cinnamon, as well as a topping of raw onions and cheese. Meanwhile, you risk being forcibly removed from Texas if you make a place for beans. The chili found in southeastern Kentucky pool halls is a different creature altogether—no beans and not overly spiced, just meat, onions and a few additions cooked down until it's ready to be scooped into a hotdog bun and served with a little mustard. The chili bun is thought to have originated in the region in the 1950s, and everyone has their favorite source. I was quickly introduced to the family tradition of stopping at Weaver's Pool Hall in London every Memorial Day weekend for a plate of chili buns before continuing on our journey to decorate graves. Rather oddly, this does seem to be a very localized dish, centered in Corbin and London and a few surrounding places. It's not high cuisine, but those who haven't tried it don't know what they are missing.

Weaver's Pool Hall in London is known for its chili buns.

2 pounds ground chuck beef
4 onions, diced
10 ounces beer
2 teaspoons salt
9 ounces can tomato puree
5 teaspoons chili powder
5 teaspoons hot sauce

Combine the ground beef chuck, onion, beer and salt in a large pan and simmer for 40 minutes, being sure to mash and break up the meat into fine pieces. Add the tomato puree, chili powder and hot sauce. Cook an additional 20 minutes. Serve on hot dog buns with mustard and onion. Can also be served over hot dogs.

PART VII

THE FUTURE OF KENTUCKY FOOD

In September 2012, I found myself sitting in a room at the Kentucky State University Research and Demonstration Farm in Frankfort, learning about the growing of pawpaws. The event was one of its monthly daylong seminars about some aspect of agriculture. This particular one had attracted far more people than expected. Staff scrambled to find more chairs, and people eagerly scribbled down notes about seasons, soil types and marketing possibilities. A few, like myself, were simply keen to learn more about how I might use the fruit. Most were farmers or gardeners, full of questions. Some had driven three or four hours to be there. Within the next month, I would find myself at two events showcasing regional foods, from bourbon balls to country ham.

In this age of convenience foods and rising obesity, it is all too easy to dismiss many of the dishes, foods and practices featured in this book as long gone, belonging to days gone by or perhaps limited only to special occasions now. To make such an assumption would be doing a great disservice to the many people throughout Kentucky who are working to retain and revitalize interest in traditional foodways. As well as an increasing interest in growing one's own food and eating organically, there is a significant movement underway in the commonwealth toward sustainable farming and preserving heirloom varieties.

One problem in eastern Kentucky has been the struggle to remain economically viable. It is difficult to compete in a market dominated by the large farming complexes of the Midwest, and many farms have now become part-time affairs, requiring the owners to seek outside employment. The Sustainable Mountain Agriculture Center is working to educate area farmers about the diversity of ways in which they can use their land and about the cultivation of traditional culture through the preservation of old crop varieties. Heirloom vegetables are not only good business, but they are also good for maintaining the nutritional and historic heritage of Kentucky. The foremost expert in collecting heirloom beans, Center president Bill Best, now has a collection of close to seven hundred varieties. Also in eastern Kentucky, Owsley County is one of the poorest counties in the nation. A joint program with the University of Kentucky has started an agricultural program at the local high school, using spare land. Students are learning about farming in the hope that it will increase the economic prospects of the county.

Such efforts are not limited to the Appalachian part of the state. Programs in the Bluegrass include Seedleaf, which utilizes a series of urban community gardens to educate children about food. Seedleaf's Soups On program uses some of the produce in an ad hoc soup kitchen, with the resulting soup being shared between the volunteers and local homeless organizations. Also in Lexington, Cooperative of Lexington Urban Chicken Keepers (CLUCK) seeks to educate local residents about raising chickens. Another recent initiative has been FoodChain, a facility that uses leftover grain from the neighboring microbrewery to raise fish and mushrooms. The fish waste is used to grow greens, while the water is recycled to feed the plants and then filtered back into the fish tanks. Everything is recycled through the chain of production and provides food for community kitchens. A next-door restaurant also makes the tilapia available to paying diners.

Meanwhile, farther west, Western Kentucky University's Office of Sustainability has partnered with the local Community Farmers Market to create the Local Food for Everyone Initiative. Mobile markets and local directories are making it easier for people in the community to support and buy from local food producers.

Kentucky is also home to a number of award-winning chefs, including Ouita Michael, Jeremy Ashby, Jonathan Lundy, Edward Lee and Anthony Lamas. These and many other statewide chefs have gained popularity for providing modern twists on traditional regional dishes, all while using local ingredients.

This book is a history of Kentucky food. You may well be asking yourself why we have now turned to look at the present and the future, and indeed you are correct. But what is the purpose of history if not to provide a means of looking forward as well as to the past? What is this history if not a celebration of Kentucky's riches? In a fictional imagining of Louisville's first Christmas, Wade Hall wrote of "meats galore…baked and fried and boiled to perfection…The corn harvested in late summer…was made into many delicious forms—corn pone, hoecake, batter cake, boiled hominy, and fried hominy." Now, if we revisit the Kentucky meal I described in this book's opening, we find country ham and fried chicken cooked to perfection, delicious corn and corn bread and a decadent array of desserts. Some of the meats may have changed, the cooking methods made easier by modern technology, but little has really changed either on or around the table. The food is still locally grown and home-cooked, and the company is still warm and inviting, ready to pull up a chair and get another plate for anyone who might happen to appear at the door.

In *Why We Eat What We Eat*, Raymond Sokolov questioned the development of American eating habits. He concluded that "America's traditional cuisine…is the result of many separate collisions between immigrant groups applying what they know from the old country to what they found in the new." So it is in Kentucky, where Scotch-Irish, English, French and German immigrants combined their know-how with that shared by the Cherokees, the Shawnees and the Chickasaws, as well as with the African traditions of the slaves. More recent influences have included Latin American, Italian, Chinese and Japanese. Given the innovation and creativity of the pioneers in Kentucky's past, we can only speculate as to how these new influences might contribute to future Kentucky cooking.

My early fears of soggy fried chicken, overcooked bland vegetables and nutritionally poor snacks have all been laid to rest by grass-fed beef, the tang of vinegar barbecue, the crunch of homegrown produce and the rich decadence of southern desserts. Given the abundance of not just good but excellent Kentucky food, one can hardly be faulted for agreeing with Thomas D. Clark:

If, beyond the pearly gates, I am permitted to select my place at the table, it will be among Kentuckians.

BIBLIOGRAPHY

Adkison, Lindsey. "A True Taste of the South.", *Brunswick News*, April 15, 2010.

Alonso, Enrique, and Ana Recarte. "Pigs in New York City: A Study on 19th Century Urban 'Sanitation.'" Case Study for the Friends of Thoreau Environmental Program, Research Institute of American Studies, University of Alcala, Spain, January 2008.

Ashe, Thomas. *Travels in America Performed in 1806*. London: Richard Phillips, 1808. Republished by Badgley Publishing Company, 2011.

Avirett, James Battle. *The Old Plantation: How We Lived in Great House and Cabin Before the War*. New York: F. Tennyson Neely Company, 1901.

Barnes, Bertha. *Rebecca Boone Cook Book*. Harlan, KY: Durham Printing, 1973.

Beattie, L. Elisabeth, ed. *Savory Memories*. Lexington: University Press of Kentucky, 1998.

Benedict, Jennie. C. *The Blue Ribbon Cook Book*. 2nd ed. Louisville, KY: John P. Morton, 1904.

Berry, Maureen. "Properly Seasoned: Embracing a Childhood Pan." *Culinate*, June 19, 2013.

Berry, Wes. *Ky BBQ*. Lexington: University Press of Kentucky, 2013.

Bitzer, Morris J. "Production of Sweet Sorghum for Syrup in Kentucky." Paper produced by the University of Kentucky College of Agriculture's Cooperative Extension Service, 1997.

Booth, Sally Smith. *Hung, Strung & Potted: A History of Eating in Colonial America*. New York: Clarkson N. Potter, 1971.

Bradley, Rose M. *The English Housewife in the Seventeenth and Eighteenth Centuries.* London: Edward Arnold, 1912.

Brown, Rodger Lyle. *Ghost Dancing on the Cracker Circuit.* Jackson: University Press of Mississippi, 1997.

Bryan, Mrs. Lettice. *The Kentucky Housewife.* Cincinnati, OH: Shepard & Stearns, 1839. Facsimile edition produced by Applewood Books, 2001.

Carruthers, Mrs. Francis. *Twentieth Century Home Cook Book.* Chicago: Thompson & Thomas, 1905.

Claiborne, Craig. *Southern Cooking.* New York: Clamshell Productions, 1987.

Clark, Thomas D. *The Kentucky.* Reprint, Lexington: University Press of Kentucky, 1992. Originally published 1942.

————. *Pills, Petticoats and Plows: The Southern Country Store.* New York: Bobbs-Merrill Company, 1944.

Cobb, Irvin S. *Cobb's Bill-of-Fare.* New York: Curtis Publishing Company, 1911.

Collier, Andrea King. "Cast Iron Skillet." *Best Food Writing 2007.* Edited by Holly Hughes. New York: Marlowe & Company, 2007.

Cooper, Dorothea, ed. *Kentucky Hospitality: A 200 Year Tradition.* Louisville: Kentucky Federation of Women's Clubs, 1976.

Cunningham, Paula, ed. *Sample West Kentucky.* Kuttawa, KY: McClanahan, 1985.

Curry, Dale. "From the Oven: Biscuits, Cornbread and Muffins." *New Orleans Magazine* (March 2011): 28–31.

Doty, William Kavanaugh. *The Confectionery of Monsieur Giron.* Charlottesville, VA: Michie Company, 1915.

Drake, Daniel. *Pioneer Life in Kentucky: 1785–1800.* New York: Henry Schuman, 1948.

Drymon, M.M. *Scotch-Irish Foodways in America.* N.p.: CreateSpace, 2009.

Dull, Mrs. S.R. *Southern Cooking.* Abridged version. New York: Grossett & Dunlap, 1977.

Edge, John T. *Fried Chicken: An American Story.* New York: G.P. Putnam's Sons, 2004.

Egerton, John. *Side Orders.* Atlanta, GA: Peachtree Publishers, 1990.

————. *Southern Food.* New York: Alfred A. Knopf, 1987.

Egerton, John, ed. *Cornbread Nation 1.* Chapel Hill: University of North Carolina Press, 2002.

Elie, Lolis Eric. *Cornbread Nation 2.* Chapel Hill: University of North Carolina Press, 2004.

Ellis, William. *A History of Education in Kentucky.* Lexington: University Press of Kentucky, 2011.

Engelhardt, Elizabeth S.D. *A Mess of Greens: Southern Gender and Southern Food.* Athens: University of Georgia Press, 2011.

Farr, Sidney Saylor. "Dried Apple Stack Cake." *Appalachian Heritage* (Fall 2004). http://community.berea.edu/appalachianheritage/issues/fall2004/memoir.html.

————. *More than Moonshine.* Pittsburgh, PA: University of Pittsburgh Press, 1983.

Fisher, Abby. *What Mrs. Fisher Knows About Southern Cooking.* San Francisco: Women's Co-op Printing Office, 1881.

Flexner, Marion. *Out of Kentucky Kitchens.* Lexington: University Press of Kentucky, 1989.

Frazer, Mary Harris. *Kentucky Receipt Book.* Louisville, KY: Bradley and Gilbert, 1903.

Fussell, Betty. *The Story of Corn.* New York: Alfred A. Knopf, 1992.

Gibbons, Euell. *Stalking the Wild Asparagus.* Chambersburg, PA: Alan C. Hood & Company, 1962.

Glasse, Hannah. *The Art of Cookery, Made Plain and Easy: Which Far Exceeds Any Thing of the Kind Yet Published.* London: publisher unknown, 1747.

Glenn, Camille. *The Heritage of Southern Cooking.* New York: Workman, 1986.

Hall, Gregory A. "Tobacco, Make Way for the Shrimp." *Cincinnati Enquirer*, June 7, 1998.

Hardeman, Nicholas P. *Shucks, Shocks and Hominy Blocks: Corn as a Way of Life in Pioneer America.* Baton Rouge: Louisiana State University Press, 1981.

Hess, John L., and Karen Hess. *The Taste of America.* New York: Grossman Publishers, 1977.

Honnert, Mark, trans. "German Pioneer Society of Covington, KY, 1877–1902." Undated. Made available by www.nkyviews.com.

Jarman, Rufus. "Please Pass the Ham." *Saturday Evening Post*, May 18, 1957, 40–41, 116–19.

Kellner, Lyn. *The Taste of Appalachia.* Boone, NC: Simmer Pot Press, 1987.

Kleber, John E., ed. *The Kentucky Encyclopedia.* Lexington: University Press of Kentucky, 1992.

Kraus, Hilary. "Southerners Take Iced Tea Seriously." *Fayetteville Observer*, July 2, 2008.

Kremer, Elizabeth C. *We Make You Kindly Welcome.* Harrodsburg, KY: Pleasant Hill Press, 1970.

Kurlansky, Mark. *The Food of a Younger Land.* New York: Riverhead Books, 2009.

Leslie, Eliza. *Directions for Cookery, in Its Various Branches.* 10th ed. Philadelphia, PA: Carey & Hart, 1840.

Lundy, Ronni. "Burgoo Bliss." *Louisville Magazine* (April 1997): 52–56.

———. *Butter Beans to Blackberries*. New York: North Point Press, 1999.

———. *Shuck Beans, Stack Cakes and Honest Fried Chicken*. New York: Atlantic Monthly Press, 1991.

Lundy, Ronni, ed. *Cornbread Nation 3*. Chapel Hill: University of North Carolina Press, 2005.

Lustig, Lillie, S. Sondheim and Sarah Rensel, eds. *The Southern Cook Book of Fine Old Recipes*. Reading, PA: Culinary Arts Press, 1935.

Lyon, George Ella, ed. *A Kentucky Christmas*. Lexington: University Press of Kentucky, 2003.

Maurer, David W. *Kentucky Moonshine*. Lexington: University Press of Kentucky, 1974.

McCulloch-Williams, Martha. *Dishes & Beverages of the Old South*. New York: McBride, Nast & Company, 1913.

McDaniel, Rick. *An Irresistible History of Southern Food: Four Centuries of Black-Eyed Peas, Collard Greens & Whole Hog Barbecue*. Charleston, SC: The History Press, 2011.

Milburn, William W. "Old-Time Sorghum Making." *Kentucky Explorer* (November 2000).

Miller, Amy Bess, and Persis Fuller. *The Best of Shaker Cooking*. New York: MacMillan, 1985.

Ozersky, Josh. *Colonel Sanders and the American Dream*. Austin: University of Texas Press, 2012.

Pegge, Samuel. "The Forme of Cury." Estimated to have been compiled in 1390. Available online at http://www.gutenberg.org/catalog/world/readfile?fk_files=3334858.

Randolph, Mary. *The Virginia Housewife*. Baltimore, MD: John Plaskitt, 1836.

Reed, Dale Volberg, and John Shelton Reed, eds. *Cornbread Nation 4*. Athens: University of Georgia Press, 2008.

Reed, Julia. *Ham Biscuits, Hostess Gowns, and Other Southern Specialties*. New York: Macmillan, 2009.

———. *Queen of the Turtle Derby and Other Southern Phenomena*. New York: Random House, 2005.

Roberts, Rona. *Sweet, Sweet Sorghum*. Lexington, KY: Hotcakes Press, 2011.

Root, Waverley, and Richard de Rochemont. *Eating in America: A History*. New York: Ecco Press, 1995.

Ross, Alice. "Cornbread—Staple of the New World." *Journal of Antiques and Collectibles* (March 2000).

———. "Corn—The Food of a Nation." *Journal of Antiques and Collectibles* (September 2000).

———. "Hunting the Welch Rabbit." *Journal of Antiques and Collectibles* (May 2000).

Ross, Elizabeth. *Cornmeal Country*. Kuttawa, KY: McClanahan, 2000.

———. *Kentucky Keepsakes*. Kuttawa, KY: McClanahan, 1996.

Sauceman, Fred W., ed. *Cornbread Nation 5*. Athens: University of Georgia Press, 2010.

Scaggs, Deirdre A., and Andrew W. McGraw. *The Historic Kentucky Kitchen*. Lexington: University Press of Kentucky, 2013.

Shackelford, Nevyle. "Most Every Family in Rural Kentucky Once Raised Chickens." *Kentucky Explorer* 28, no. 3 (August 2013).

Simmons, Amelia. *American Cookery, or the Art of Dressing….* Hartford, CT: Hudson & Goodwin, 1796. Now available online at http://www.gutenberg.org/cache/epub/12815/pg12815.html.

Smith, Bob. "'Taters' Were a Mainstay for the Folks of Appalachia." *Kentucky Explorer* 28, no. 3 (August 2013).

Sohn, Mark F. *Appalachian Home Cooking: History, Culture, and Recipes*. Lexington: University Press of Kentucky, 2005.

———. *Mountain Country Cooking*. New York: St. Martin's Press, 1996.

Sokolov, Raymond. *Why We Eat What We Eat*. New York: Summit Books, 1991.

Spaulding, Lily May, and John Spaulding, eds. *Civil War Recipes: Receipts from the Pages of Godey's Lady's Book*. Lexington: University Press of Kentucky, 1999.

Spence, Carol Lea. "There's No Business Like Sheep Business." *Kentucky Forward*, August 31, 2013. http://www.kyforward.com/2013/08/theres-no-business-like-sheep-business-as-kentucky-producers-tap-into-rich-history.

Spencer, Colin. *British Food: An Extraordinary Thousand Years of History*. New York: Columbia University Press, 2003.

Stoddart, Jess. *Challenge and Change in Appalachia*. Lexington: University of Kentucky Press, 2002.

Sturtz, James. "Meat." *Best Food Writing 2007*. Edited by Holly Hughes. New York: Marlowe & Company, 2007.

Trillin, Calvin. *Alice, Lets Eat*. New York: Random House, 2007.

Tyree, Marion Cabell. *Housekeeping in Old Virginia*. Louisville, KY: John P. Morton & Company, 1878.

Van Willigen, John, and Anne van Willigen. *Food and Everyday Life on Kentucky Family Farms, 1920–1950*. Lexington: University of Kentucky Press, 2006.

Weinzweig, Ari. "Potlikker: From Slave Plantations to Today." *The Atlantic*, April 16, 2009. http://www.theatlantic.com/health/archive/2009/04/potlikker-from-slave-plantations-to-today/7129.

White, Joyce. "The Art of Southern Fried Chicken." *New York Amsterdam News*, May 12, 2005, 26.

Wilcox, Estelle Woods. *Buckeye Cookery and Practical Housekeeping.* Marysville, OH: Buckeye Publishing Company, 1877.

INDEX

A

African influence 15, 28, 32, 68, 134
Ale-8-One 92
apples 50, 52, 53, 103

B

bananas 110, 111
barbecue 60, 64
beans 12, 31, 32, 133
  black-eyed peas 36
  leatherbritches 32
beer cheese 127, 128
Benedictine 129
Benedict, Jennie 97, 129
Bibb, John 41
biscuits 20, 22, 29, 97, 99, 100
bourbon 14, 114, 119
  mint julep 84, 85
  Old Fashioned 86
burgoo 12, 60

C

cabbage 34, 35, 36, 38, 39, 40
cakes
  Bible Cake 106
  Coca-Cola Cake 107
  Jam Cake 106
  Lincoln Cake 116
  Pound Cake 101, 102
  Spice Cake 97
  Stack Cake 103
candy 96, 115, 120
  Bourbon Balls 120
  Divinity 121
chicken 67, 70, 71, 133
chili 130
corn 9, 12, 14, 15, 22, 23, 25, 28, 30,
    32, 54, 80, 98
  corn bread 24, 25, 26, 27
  grits 29
  hoecakes 12
  spoonbread 28
country ham 15, 56
custard 109

D

Derby 84, 125
Dutch influence 15, 39

E

eggnog 109
English influence 14, 41, 45, 51, 67,
    84, 101, 109, 112, 134

F

fish 73, 74, 133
French influence 15, 28, 67, 75, 134
frog legs 75

G

German influence 15, 32, 39, 42, 48,
    126, 128
Giron, Mathurin 115
goetta 126
gravy 59, 71, 100
greens 12, 35, 36, 38, 39
  poke 12, 37

H

Hines, Duncan 68, 108
Hot Brown 122

I

iced tea 88, 89, 90

L

lettuce 41, 42

M

moonshine 15, 86, 87, 88
morels 43
mutton 16, 62, 64, 65

N

Native American influence 23, 28, 32,
    43, 44, 115

O

oysters 60, 78

P

pawpaw 49, 50, 132
pies 17, 45, 50, 112, 114, 125

pork 15, 16, 34, 36, 54, 55, 58, 62,
    64, 65, 126
potatoes 45, 48, 120
pot likker 27, 36, 38

R

ramps 43
Rebecca-Ruth Candy 117, 118, 119
Ruth Hunt 119

S

Sanders, Harland 68, 69, 70
Scotch-Irish 12, 47
Shakers 15, 48
sorghum 17, 93, 96, 103
squash 12, 21, 44
  cushaw 44, 45
  pumpkin 44, 45

ABOUT THE AUTHOR

Although a Brit by birth, Fiona Young-Brown has been a Kentucky resident for thirteen years, during which time she has developed a love of bourbon and an appreciation for iced tea and corn bread. She is the author of two other books, including Wicked Lexington, and is a member of the American Society of Journalists and Authors. When not writing, Fiona is busy traveling, researching genealogy or cooking for her food blog, www.crazyenglishwomancooks.com. She lives in Lexington with her Clay County–born husband, Nic, and their two dogs.

Visit us at
www.historypress.net
....
This title is also available as an e-book